Nancy J. Cohen

Writing the Cozy Mystery

WRITING THE COZY MYSTERY, Second Edition

Published November 2018 by Orange Grove Press
Printed in the United States of America

Digital ISBN: 978-0-9985317-2-4
Print ISBN: 978-0-9985317-3-1
Cover Design and Graphic Illustrations by Boulevard Photografica
Digital Layout by www.formatting4U.com

Table of Contents

Introduction

One of the best ways to begin writing mysteries is to read them. If you gravitate toward a certain type of story, likely that is the subgenre you'll pursue as a writer. Are you attracted to bright, cheery covers with funny titles or to more serious works? In your crime fiction, do you read books that delve into the psychology of a criminal, or would you rather choose a lighthearted whodunit?

Despite market fluctuations, cozy mysteries have always been popular. Readers like cozies because they offer an escape from reality. Unlike the real world where criminals often go free and victims lack justice, in a cozy the crook is always caught and the sleuth emerges unharmed. The focus is more on the puzzle of solving the mystery than the forensics. These stories satisfy our need for justice and a happy ending.

How do you write a cozy mystery? In this book, you'll learn to how develop your characters, build your setting, plot the story, add suspense, and sustain your series.

This Second Edition contains expanded sections; more examples; additional writing exercises; and seven new chapters, including The Muddle in the Middle, Romance and Murder, Special Considerations for Cozy Writers, Keeping a Series Fresh, Writing the Smart Synopsis, Mystery Movies, and Marketing Tips. Also, questions such as these are answered:

Can I use real places?
Does the crime have to be a murder?

How many suspects are a good number?
When should the dead body show up?
How can you avoid police involvement?
What is a Red Herring?
What types of questions must be resolved by the end of the story?
How important is originality?
Can serious issues be included in a cozy?

Most examples in this book are from my own work simply for the sake of expediency. Let's begin by taking a closer look at genre definitions.

Chapter One – Defining the Genre

Traditional mysteries are akin to Agatha Christie novels, wherein the puzzle is the thing. Readers expect to solve a crime along with the sleuth. A cozy is a type of traditional mystery.

A cozy mystery can be defined as a whodunit featuring an amateur sleuth, a distinctive setting, and a limited number of suspects, most of whom know each other and have a motive for murder. These stories contain no explicit sex, violence, or bad language. For the most part, they are "clean" books that can be read by all ages. As one reader said, "I love a good mystery with no obscenities, smut or gory details."

Humor is often evident in cozies (as witnessed by the "punny" titles), and so are recipes. Pets, crafts, and culinary skills are welcome, but don't kill the favored cat or dog. While murder is usually the basis for the story, the focus of a cozy is on interpersonal relationships rather than crime scene details or lab results. Readers who don't like to be frightened know they will get a lighthearted story with a challenging puzzle, interesting characters, and a view of a world they might not experience otherwise.

These novels center on the connections among individuals, and not on large, impersonal groups like global terrorists, international drug cartels, or secret government agencies. Those are reserved for thrillers that deal with a broader scope. Psychological studies of the criminal mind or profiles of serial killers don't play a big role here either. These would more likely be seen in suspense novels. Police procedurals, detective stories, and courtroom dramas are other subgenres of the mystery field.

In a cozy, the sleuth's world is just as important as solving the murder. We read these stories to learn about a new occupation or to vicariously explore a different locale. Readers like to follow the sleuth's personal life, which is the key to bringing fans back for the next installment. Be prepared for the long haul with your characters and setting, because readers as well as editors prefer series.

The amateur sleuth is your average Joe or Joanne. This person is not professionally engaged in hunting down or prosecuting criminals. The sleuth may run into serious danger but isn't physically damaged to any great extent.

Occupations of today's protagonists range from bakery owners to antique dealers to real estate agents to caterers. Popular subcategories include culinary cozies, animal mysteries (i.e. pets), cozy craft and hobby mysteries. Paranormal mysteries may include ghosts or other supernatural elements, while historical mysteries always attract a following. Don't be afraid if your story doesn't fit into one of these subsets. Readers are always looking for something new and fresh, and so are editors.

An example of a cozy series on television is *Murder, She Wrote* with Angela Lansbury, who played mystery writer and amateur sleuth Jessica Fletcher. She lived in the small town of Cabot Cove, Maine, and solved murders on a weekly basis. Then there's the entertaining *Mystery Woman* series of Hallmark TV movies starring Kellie Martin as bookstore owner Samantha Kinsey. An avid mystery fan, Samantha gets caught up in solving crimes as much as bookselling. Look at the Hallmark Movies and Mysteries Channel for more TV series in this genre: http://www.hallmarkmoviesandmysteries.com/.

The classic *Clue* game offers another example of a murder happening in a confined setting with a limited number of suspects. Throw in a few secrets and motives for murder, and you have a classic cozy. An entire conference, Malice Domestic, is devoted to the traditional mystery genre. This shows you how many devoted fans are out there, waiting for your book. For more information on this event, visit http://www.malicedomestic.org.

The Eight C's of Cozy Mysteries are depicted in this graphic, although all of these items are neither required nor exclusive. It's my fun take on the genre.

Chapter Two – World Building

How do you establish setting?

Decide what ambiance you want to impart with your series and select a locale to reflect this lifestyle. Will it be a seaside village, a mountain ski resort, a coastal New England town, or a flashy city? These surroundings will take on characteristics of their own as you map out your territory, add regional flavors, and throw in some local slang.

Plan to lay the groundwork for your series in book one. Although your heroine's adventures will be ongoing, each story should stand alone and come to a satisfactory conclusion. It's the evolving personal relationships among the recurrent characters that will propel readers to your next book. In the meantime, be sure your setting allows for people to come and go, as you'll need a new set of suspects for each story.

Also, when some of your continuing characters leave the stage, you may want to bring others onboard. So even though you might set your series in a small town, create a canvas large enough to accommodate an influx of new blood.

My Bad Hair Day mysteries are set in sunny South Florida. Balmy breezes, sun-kissed sand, and beautiful beaches bring to mind a lazy tropical setting under the sizzling sun. But the heat can act like a flame to ignite boiling passions, inspiring murder and mayhem.

Florida life suits me, and I want to share my enjoyment of the rich, earthy scent of humus, the graceful sight of palm fronds swaying in a breeze, the blazing tangerine sunsets, and the seductive fragrance of gardenia blossoms. I hope to convey the tart taste of Key lime pie, the sweetness of fresh-squeezed orange juice, and the honeyed flavor of homegrown bananas.

Marla Shore, my hairdresser sleuth, lives in the fictional town of Palm Haven located between Fort Lauderdale and the Everglades. As part of the South Florida melting pot of immigrants and northern transplants, its population can be diverse, although residents of this community tend to be more affluent. An upscale suburban community, Palm Haven is lushly landscaped and boasts an above-average income level for its residents. However, behind the manicured lawns lurk secrets that can be dark and deadly.

South Florida has a lot to offer beyond its beaches, including varied ecological systems and hot topic issues. Writing mysteries set in this locale gives me an excuse to explore this steamy environment.

What slice of life do you want to showcase? Once you select your setting, you're committed for the length of the series. So make sure it's a place you enjoy and one that comes with its own set of conflicts beneath the surface.

Can I use real places?

Yes, if nothing bad happens there. Then you'll want to change the name. If two people are chatting while sipping tea, you can name the restaurant. But beware that restaurants go out of business and then your work will appear dated. As for the name of your town, if you use a real place, everything has to be accurate. Whereas if you make up a location, you can move buildings around, add parks and community halls, or lay out the interior of the police station the way you want it.

Readers do like to recognize locales, so if you sprinkle in enough real sites, they'll be excited and pleased. As one reader said to me, "Having lived in Broward County, I loved reading about all the places that were home to me. It gave me lots of warm fuzzies." Or another: "I grew up down in that area. As I read though the book, it was like I was there. Thanks for the tour of memory lane."

Florida is a magnet for readers and writers alike. Our varied demographics, diverse ecology, and wealth of social issues lend fodder for stories, while tourists like to mentally revisit places they've been or would like to see. So think carefully about what you'd like to include for real and what you'd like to make up.

Narrow the details.

What makes your setting distinctive? How do these factors impact your story? Consider the following once you've determined your general setting. If you're writing a historical mystery, these details are even more important to research accurately.

Activities of Daily Living—Jobs, work hours, chores, meal times, sleep habits.
Ecology—Climate, plants, pollution, weather, wildlife, environmental concerns.
Economics—What is the town's economic level? Your character's situation?
Education—Educational levels, teachers and mentors, school system.
Entertainment—What do your characters enjoy for recreation in their spare time?
Food—Meal preparation, food staples, dining establishments, cultural practices.
Geography—Geological terrain, forests, lakes, mountains, oceans.
Government—Political structure, local conflicts, power influencers.
Housing—Architecture, construction, design, furnishings and accessories.

Language—Speech patterns, favorite phrases, local slang.
Legal System—Judges, court system, police department, sheriff's office.
Medical—Holistic or traditional medicine? Herbal meds or prescribed drugs?
Physical Characteristics—Facial features, hair texture, body build, mode of dress.
Religion—Special foods, holidays, and rituals.
Social Relationships—Family units, courtship rituals, sexual attitudes.
Technology—Determine how your characters use the technology of the era.
Transportation—How does your character's means of transport reflect his personality?

Bring in the five senses.

To make the story come alive for readers, you'll want to add sensory details to help them see, smell, taste, feel, and hear the place where your characters live. These factors are critically important for making your story seem real. Ditto for your sleuth's profession. Do your research to make these details richly authentic for your fans. Then you'll get responses like these: "What I like about your books is that I can actually smell in my mind the hair color solutions and the hair spray." Or, "I have been a hairdresser for over 30 years and you have such a knowledge of our profession that I thought you had roots in hairdressing."

Be careful not to let your research show too much, however. All descriptions should be observed by your viewpoint character. What is her emotional response? Does a certain smell bring back a memory or provide a sense of comfort? Is your heroine unaccustomed to wearing heels and afraid of tripping on the bumpy sidewalk? Does she hate the humidity for how it frizzes her hair or love how it moisturizes her skin? We see the world through our own lenses. So should your sleuth.

Whenever you travel or go on a research trip, take notes and photos to help remind you of these sensory impressions later. They're more important than the sites you visit. You can look up places online, but you won't find the spicy scent you smelled in the air, the uneven pavement underfoot with weeds growing in the cracks, the sounds coming from someone pressure cleaning his roof, the yellow wildflowers by the roadside, or the heavy moisture that fills your lungs. These exquisite details are what you need to scatter amongst your scenes.

Setting within a Setting

As mystery writers, we are trained to place our sleuths within a distinctive milieu that becomes a character in itself. Whether it's a small town, a neighborhood in a big city, or a regional locale, this setting imbues our stories with a unique flavor. We assign an occupation to our sleuth that further defines this world.

For each story, we need to add another layer. Think of concentric circles each enclosing the other with the sleuth in the center. In watching traditional mysteries on TV, I've noticed how each show focuses on a narrow group of people, same as we do in a cozy mystery. It's easier to plot the story when we pick a setting with built-in suspects.

As an example, tune in to "The Brokenwood Mysteries" on the Acorn Channel featuring Detective Senior Sergeant Mike Shepherd (Neill Rea) and Detective Constable Kristin Sims (Fern Sutherland). Although this show is a police procedural, the focus rests on the interpersonal relationships among the characters same as in a cozy. Each episode takes place at a setting within a setting. Check it out here: http://thebrokenwoodmysteries.com/

Besides the larger scope of Brokenwood, New Zealand, these stories center on a wine tasting competition, a hunting expedition, a country club for golfers, a mansion with contestants playing a live Clue game, a classic car show, a country western concert, and a tour group. It's fun to watch the clues unfold amidst the humor and friendly banter among the main characters.

Each setting provides its own group of suspects. So choose your overall series milieu and then pick where each particular story is going to take place.

For book one, you'll want to introduce the sleuth and the recurrent characters without going too far astray. But for book two, you can vary the secondary location. For example, *Permed to Death*, #1 in my Bad Hair Day series, focuses on Marla's hair salon. We're introduced to hairstylist Marla Shore right before her client dies in the shampoo chair while getting a perm.

Hair Raiser, book #2, takes the action to Cousin Cynthia's seaside estate. Cynthia, who volunteers for an ocean preservation society, asks Marla for help when their upcoming fundraiser is sabotaged. *Murder by Manicure* switches the scene to a day spa. And so on. The background action still takes place at Marla's salon, but the mystery involves a different group of people for each installment.

The best thing about this technique is that you get a ready set of suspects. Are you featuring a writer's conference where the diva gets knocked off? Suspects can include a bunch of envious writers, the diva's agent, her editor, her publicist, and even some fanatic fans. One of these people could be her secret lover. Another person could be the past colleague whose work she ripped off. Then again, maybe the diva's best friend who writes for the same publisher will get more attention now that she's out of the way.

You see how each person has a motive? Next you link them together as you'll see below.

How do you keep track of these details?

Consider starting a series bible. In this document, you can include a map of your town, the street where your sleuth lives and/or works, and any particular locations that feature into your series as a whole. Put together a photo collage of your protagonist's lifestyle in terms of clothing, hobbies, and other interests. Or do a collage for the locale. You can even start a Pinterest story board to share with readers. Make sure you use royalty-free images to avoid copyright issues and read the terms carefully. Note the timelines for your series, including character birthdays and ages for each installment. List names of pets and housing developments, the type of car your sleuth drives, and any other detail you might need to recall for a future book. Later on we'll talk about Plotting Notebooks that can be helpful in this regard.

Historical Mysteries

You might have to dig deeper to research historical details. Primary sources such as old maps, newspapers, magazines, and diaries can be helpful. Visiting the setting can provide sensory details as well as travel blogs. Read other mysteries set in the era so you get a sense of the time period and the language in use back then. Be careful of slang phrases and check when they originated.

Since the focus of cozies remains on interpersonal relationships, you don't have to delve into forensics. It doesn't matter when fingerprinting, DNA analysis, or criminal profiling came into play unless these methods figure into your story. Instead, the sleuth must rely on her instincts, physical clues, observations, and interviews.

Can you use real historical figures that are dead? Yes, since liability laws refer to living people. There are many mysteries out there featuring famous persons from the past. But be aware that their descendants might still be around, so don't deviate too much from the truth.

When a historical figure is your main character, try to keep as close to actual history as possible, such as where they went on certain dates. If you make them secondary characters, on the other hand, then you have more literary license to be creative.

Either way, incorporate their true personality traits, beliefs, modes of dress and other details to give them authenticity.

Example

Here's a map of **Sugar Crest Plantation Resort** in *Dead Roots*. Marla brings her fiancé, Detective Dalton Vail, to a family reunion at this haunted Florida resort. As if dealing with her relatives isn't enough, a body turns up over Thanksgiving weekend.

How did I develop this site? I used *Haunt Hunter's Guide to Florida* by Joyce Elson Moore to research haunted sites in Florida and local ghost stories. Then I watched Disney's *Tower of Terror* movie starring Steve Guttenberg and Kirsten Dunst. In this film, the Hollywood Tower Hotel is haunted by a past tragedy. The protagonists must unravel this mystery to put the spirits to rest.

Personal visits to plantation sites and historic hotels, combined with these resources, inspired my imaginary resort. Ghosts and paranormal investigators are part of the weekend. I wish this place were real so I could stay there!

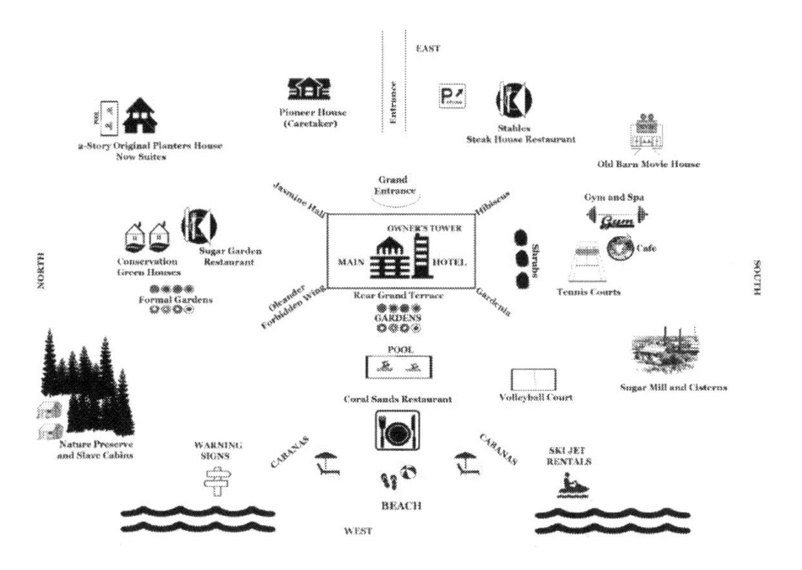

Writing Exercise

Decide where your series will take place. Why did you choose this location? What is unique about it? How can you get these qualities across to readers? What are some sensory details that you can use? How does your sleuth fit into this milieu? Where will each mystery take place within this larger scope?

Chapter Three – Creating the Sleuth

How do you establish your protagonist?

In selecting your sleuth's occupation, you'll offer the reader a glimpse into a world that might be new and different. Do your research and include job-oriented details and references to immerse the reader in this unique environment. Make sure it's a job you're comfortable researching. If you know more about kitchens than Krebs cycles, make your heroine a chef, not a biologist.

Your protagonist should be in a situation that brings her into contact with many people, or else her social circle must provide the same purpose. If she has a job, she is able to get time off to investigate the crime while still running errands and doing chores like the rest of us. She has to be real to you before she can be believable to the reader.

As for personality traits, her skills of observation complement her intelligence and sharp wit. She is compelled to seek the truth, to boldly go where no one so committed has gone before. A determined woman, she is inquisitive, assertive, and independent. Yet she's also a good listener, meaning other characters want to confide in her.

She isn't TSTL—Too Stupid to Live—so she won't go into a dark basement where the killer is hiding unless she suspects someone else of being the culprit or believes the situation to be harmless. She may look for the best in people, but she questions her assumptions when obvious clues fly in her face.

Having a sense of humor is a bonus and works well in a mystery series. But while incorporating a humorous slant into your stories, don't lose sight of the fact that people are grieving after the loss of a loved one. The effect of a murder on the victim's family shouldn't be slighted. It's easier when the victim is a person nobody likes, because then lots of folks may have wanted to see that person dead.

Your sleuth should have flaws as well as strengths. If she has an internal emotional issue that affects her behavior, this allows for character growth and subplots that increase story depth. A particular phobia—like heights, tight spaces, spiders, or public speaking—might challenge her ability to investigate the crime, making it necessary for her to confront her fears and rise above them. Past mistakes can come back to haunt her. Old flames can reappear to complicate her social life. Bad relationships in the past may prevent her from moving forward with a new love interest. Determine what caused these issues and how they influence current reactions to events.

Also establish the sleuth's short and long term goals. What does she want now? How about five years ahead? Maybe her short-term goal is to become financially independent. Long term, she yearns to travel and see the world. How does she plan to achieve these goals? Why does she want them? What's holding her back from achieving her heart's desire?

Give your character a concrete symbol of her ultimate dream. Perhaps you have a hero who wants to sail the world. Since owning a boat is his dream, he carries a tattered photo of this vessel in his pocket. Remember the hero's yacht at the end of *Romancing the Stone*? Why was achieving this goal so important to him?

Your protagonist should have a personal reason for wanting to solve the murder. Upping the personal stakes creates tension and snags the reader's interest. If your sleuth cares, so will your readers. What's at stake for your sleuth if the killer roams free and the crime isn't solved? Let us know the main character's personal goals, what led her to them, and why she's having trouble achieving them. Create two threads, one for the crime scene and one for your sleuth as a person. Weave these together throughout the story for added depth.

What is Conflict?

Internal conflict is the struggle within a character. This concerns personal problems that the protagonist must overcome. These motivating factors influence the heroine's actions. *External conflict* involves outside forces such as villainy, acts of nature, or war. In a cozy, the external conflict is the murder mystery.

Examples of Internal Conflicts from Films

Lord of the Rings

- Son seeks approval and recognition from a father who favors his brother.
- Man struggles against the pull of corruption.
- Woman wants to fight in a world that belongs to Man.
- Woman loves man who loves another woman.
- Woman must give up her special power to be with the man she loves.
- Man fears he will succumb to the same weakness as his father.

Battlestar Galactica TV series remake

- Man blames his father for the death of his brother. The father yearns for forgiveness and love from his remaining child.
- A rebellious female pilot saves the hero with her skill and daring, but she can't admit she cares for him. If she shows her soft side, she might lose the crew's respect.
- A man who traded sex for industrial secrets and caused the Earth's destruction is driven by guilt and the need for redemption.

- A weak, drunken executive officer is unable to make command decisions as he struggles against his alcohol addiction.

Bad Hair Day Mysteries

Hairstylist Marla Shore harbors guilt from a past tragedy. When she was a teenager, she babysat for a toddler who drowned in a backyard pool while under her care. She seeks redemption and self-forgiveness, and this partially motivates her actions in solving crimes. She couldn't save the child back then, but she can help murder victims find justice now.

Because of this incident, Marla fears the loss of a loved one if she has children and lacks confidence in her mothering ability. For these reasons, she doesn't want kids. In addition, she fears loss of independence if she remarries. Her first husband, Stan, was a domineering man who always put her down.

Detective Dalton Vail still grieves for his dead wife. He hasn't changed anything in his house since she died. He has a twelve-year-old daughter and won't accept advice on raising teenagers. Having lost his wife to cancer, he is afraid of losing Marla. He wants to protect her, but she keeps placing herself in jeopardy. She interprets his protective behavior as telling her what to do.

In order for them to progress in their relationship, they have to overcome these hang-ups. For each two steps forward they take, they fall back one. It's a slow progress but each book in the series shows a positive momentum. We'll look at some examples later.

Finally, they get married in book ten. Does this mean the series should end? Not at all. Like in real marriages, they'll still have issues to confront, such as raising a teenager who's learning how to drive, dealing with in-laws, and adjusting to their new life together. If we always have problems to encounter, why shouldn't your characters?

Useful aids in character development can include the

Character Development Tool, your character's Life Space, an interview with the protagonist, or a "Day in the Life" written in her viewpoint, all of which are discussed below.

Resources

GMC: Goal, Motivation, and Conflict by Debra Dixon
The Writer's Journey: Mythic Structure for Writers by Christopher Vogler
Michael Hauge's site at http://www.storymastery.com/

Character Development Tool

NAME:

JOB TITLE & EDUCATION:

PHYSICAL FEATURES:

FAVORITE SPEECH PHRASES:

LIFESTYLE (clothing, residence, leisure activities, significant others):

GOAL (What does your character need or want?):

MOTIVES (Why is this goal important?):

CONFLICT (What is obstructing the path?):

DARK SECRET:

RULING PASSION: (i.e. music, art, spreading goodwill, saving the environment)

STRENGTHS:

FLAWS: (i.e. unable to say no to friends)

DOMINANT TRAIT: (Non-physical adjective + decision-making noun – i.e. a stubborn loner or a flighty dreamer or a caring nurturer)

GROWTH AND CHANGE:

Character Arcs

In a cozy series, your characters need to transform. The sleuth can grow and change toward an overall series arc at a slow pace, but each story should have its own resolution, not only of the mystery, but also of the protagonist's mindset. This involves the sleuth's internal conflicts, which you've set up beginning with book one. She needs to have some hang-ups at the start that can be overcome throughout the course of a series. This is the overall character arc. For each title, this person also needs to come to an insight about herself by the end of the book.

Yes, there are series—like Nancy Drew—whose characters don't change. Some heroines can't seem to make a choice between suitors, or their outlook doesn't alter much from book to book. I quickly get annoyed with these people and stop reading after a few stories. What really attracts readers are the personal developments. They want to see what's going to happen next to your main character.

If you want to grip readers, your protagonist should have a journey of self-realization. It can be a small change per book, but you want an emotional impact beyond the puzzle of the crime. Emotional resonance comes from conflict. Your character can't resolve this internal conflict without some sort of behavioral change.

Think about the series you follow avidly. What brings you back to those stories and that world? Here are some sample character arcs:

- Redemption
- Forgiveness of oneself or another
- From no interest in life to a reason for living
- Beauty comes from within
- Moving from dependence to self-reliance
- Accepting another's flaws
- Learning to yield control in love

- Accepting oneself
- Rebounding from disaster
- Seeing reality instead of viewing the world as one wishes to see it
- Learning to be optimistic in the face of adversity
- Expanding one's viewpoint
- Accepting responsibility
- Admitting one isn't always right

To get inside your sleuth's head, draw her Life Space. Start with a circle and write her name in it. Then add cartoon-like bubbles around her head. Inside of these bubbles, put her concerns at any given moment in time. What's on her mind right now? This will provide insight into your character's interests.

You can also write "A Day in the Life" from her viewpoint and have her tell us what's going on that day. This will help you express her inner voice. Save this piece as a blog article for when you are promoting your book. See Dru's Book Musings for examples at https://drusbookmusing.com/.

Here is an example of Marla's Life Space in *Permed to Death:*

Marla's Life Space
in
PERMED TO DEATH

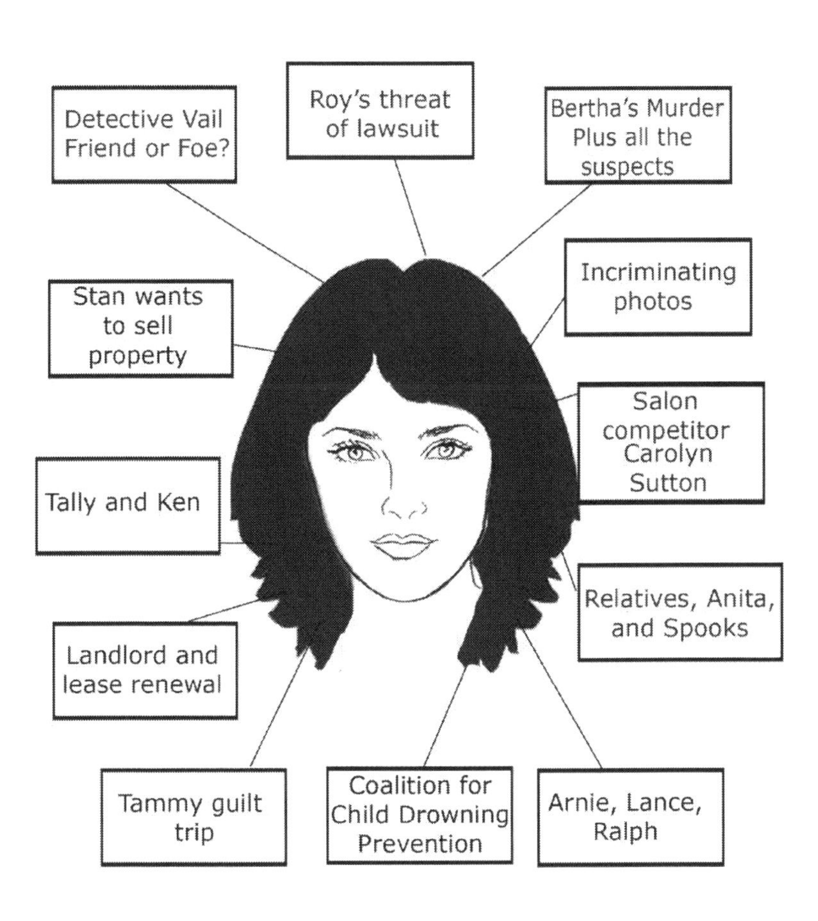

Interview your sleuth to get a feeling for how she reacts and how she talks. Laying this groundwork will give you a glimpse into her personality. You don't have to write extensive biographies about your characters, but you will want to know their basic educational level and other relevant data. Consider the world building details above. For example, what are your character's favorite foods? Guilty pleasures? Cultural specialties? Favorite holidays? Does she like to cook or prefer to grab fast food? Or does she enjoy fine dining?

You'll get to know your people in more depth as you write the story. Just remember to jot down the details of their lives so you can be consistent throughout the series.

Male versus Female Protagonists

Since most cozy readers are women, fans are comfortable with female sleuths. That's not to say you can't have a male protagonist in a cozy mystery. Certainly women read books with male leads. You can have a male sleuth in a cozy setting as long as you follow genre conventions. Add in some humor and romance, and you'll draw an audience.

If you're a male writer, be sensitive to the feminine viewpoint. It'll show in how you portray your women characters. Also keep in mind that readers want to learn about the hero's life outside of his sleuthing.

Put "cozy mysteries male protagonist" into the search window at Amazon, and a slew of titles will pop up. It can be just as fun to read a cozy with a male sleuth.

First Person or Third Person Viewpoint

Many cozies use first person viewpoint, but this is not a requirement. You can write in third person point of view (POV) as long as the reader follows along in one character's head. What does this mean?

First person viewpoint uses "I" and "me" as in, *I stepped*

forward and then froze at the sight ahead. My heart skipped a beat. Could that be... no, surely it wasn't a severed hand. A few yards farther lay a woman's body. Realizing the killer might still be around, I glanced at the open doorway to the next room. Oh, heavens. Was that a rustle I'd just heard?

In contrast, third person viewpoint uses "She" and "her" as in, *She stepped forward and then froze at the sight ahead. Her heart skipped a beat. Could that be... no, surely it wasn't a severed hand. A few yards farther lay a woman's body. Realizing the killer might still be around, she glanced at the open doorway to the next room. Oh, heavens. Was that a rustle she'd just heard?*

Both give a sense of immediacy. Whichever method you choose, keep in mind that the reader and the sleuth must solve the mystery together. You cannot leave the protagonist's head and bounce into someone else's mind. The reader only sees what the sleuth does.

Watch your Timing

In most cases, you won't want your characters to age at the same rate as you publish your novels. Space the stories several months apart to slow the aging process. Keep a timeline for each book, so you know how old the people are from one story to the next. For kids, write down what grade they're in to keep track of this detail. Assign birthdays to your characters so you'll remember, depending on what season your book takes place in, if a celebration is in order.

Recurrent Secondary Characters

The continuing cast springs from the background setting, which includes your sleuth's professional contacts, her neighbors, and her relatives. Examine your main character's friends, family, and business associates. Which one can serve as a sounding board for your protagonist? In a mystery, it's helpful to appoint a sidekick who can review suspects with your sleuth. In another genre, this role might be filled by a mentor who provides a broader perspective or suggests a new course of action.

A minor character can be grouchy or make you laugh; can act as a fool or a foil to the protagonist; can be a serious confidant or a fun-loving airhead. Modes of dress, mannerisms, speech, and attitudes should reflect the uniqueness of the individual. You'll want your supporting cast of characters to be interesting and quirky so as to provide entertaining diversion throughout a series. Some of them may become victims in future novels. Others may provide reasons for your sleuth's personal involvement in solving the crime. Some may be on stage during each installment, while others may show up from time to time. Their goals and conflicts might provide subplots that last through several stories.

While you can introduce new characters in subsequent books, your readers will be looking to the recurrent cast for a feeling of welcome. They will become interested in the lives of these people and how they interact with your protagonist. This immersion in your imaginary world will propel them to buy the subsequent story to see what happens next to your heroine.

This factor is critically important to the success of your series. You want to create people readers will care about and who they will root for during the ups and downs of life. Make your characters real. Give them problems and show us how they overcome them. Have their relationships with the people who surround them grow and change like they do in reality. Give your characters choices to make. Have them make some bad decisions but move on to better themselves. Make these people friends we'd like to meet in real life.

Marla, my hairstylist sleuth, owns and operates a hair salon in Palm Haven, Florida. Ask around and see if you can find anyone who has not stepped inside a salon for a cut, color, or styling. It's a great setting for a mystery series because people come and go, exchange gossip, and confide in their hairdressers. Despite Marla's busy schedule, she still finds time to investigate murders.

Recurrent characters include her colleagues, friends, family members, and neighbors. Regarding Marla's hair salon clients, some may be suspects while others provide information. Scenes set in the beauty shop further the plot and reveal glimpses into Marla's character. As you can see, the setting becomes an integral part of your characters while acting as the springboard for their creation.

Subplots

A romantic subplot is welcome along with the ensuing sexual sizzle, as long as any overt bedroom scenes take place off-stage. This subplot can involve your sleuth and a love interest, or it can happen between two secondary characters. Or there could be a love triangle until your sleuth makes up her mind which suitor she favors.

However, not every cozy writer feels comfortable writing romance. That's fine, but you'll need something else to fill the gap. Maybe your sleuth has a terrible boss, or there's a mean girl at work. Or she has problems with her sibling or a parent. These are all part of the internal conflicts that give your characters added depth.

In my series, Marla is harangued by her mother, Anita, to date a Jewish optometrist who is the son of Anita's boyfriend. The latter fellow is a boisterous type whom Marla dislikes. Then there's her brother, who she doesn't call as often as she should. At work, her friend Nicole has problems with a commitment-phobic boyfriend. Plus, Marla is forced to deal with staffing problems at the salon. These relationships change as the series evolves.

Just like friends in real life, people come and go as subjects for subplots. These characters help to showcase our protagonist's life as she responds to the situation. Here are some suggestions that you might use in your story:

Romance

- Between man and woman
- Old flame returns to town

Love triangle
Between secondary characters
Family
Sibling who always gets in trouble
Sick child, rebellious child, competitive child
Father/son issues, Mother/daughter issues
Holidays or Celebrations can cause tensions to rise
Work
Bad boss
Mean co-worker
Competition for promotion
Project deadline
Housing/Neighbor Issues
Financial Issues

Writing Exercise

Tell us about your heroine. What does she do for a living? Why does that occupation appeal to her? What does she want to accomplish? Why is this goal important to her? What obstacles stand in her path? How does she plan to achieve her heart's desire? Does she have a dark secret that holds her back? Or a hidden passion that she can't deny?

What qualities does she possess that will make her a good sleuth? Who are the secondary characters that will be with her throughout the series? What issues will they bring to the story?

Now write a scene describing her day using first person and third person viewpoint. Which POV feels more natural to you?

Chapter Four – A Web of Suspects

Select a Victim

You may already have a victim in mind based on the setting of your story. Who do you want to kill off? The nasty principal in the local school? The lazy whiner at work? Miserly Aunt Harriet? Your deadbeat husband? Or maybe the respected keynote speaker at a writers' conference?

We'll worry about *why* later—that's where passion comes into play. Right now, you're just identifying the soon-to-be deceased. If your sleuth already knows the victim, that's even better. It gives her a compelling reason to get involved, which in turn raises the emotional stakes and makes readers care about what happens.

Be careful about killing off a favorite character. If you have to get rid of someone, knock off a minor player. Nothing will infuriate readers more than if you build anticipation about a love interest and then you murder this person. They want to anticipate a happy payoff at the finale. There are other ways to get rid of someone, like job transfers or a falling out in a relationship.

Establish the Crime Scene

When writing a cozy mystery, you need to decide upon crime scene details even though interpersonal relations, and not forensics, are your story's focus. Here's an example of what this means. For *Trimmed to Death*, my work-in-progress as of this writing, I decided to set the scene at a bake-off contest held at Kinsdale Farms during their harvest festival. Now what? Think about the five W's when you're in this plotting phase.

Who ends up dead? [Spoiler Alert] Let's say Francine Dodger, one of the contestants, is the victim. She's also the quarry in the Find Franny live scavenger hunt at the festival.

Where is the person killed? Marla finds the woman's body out in a strawberry field. Was Francine lured to this site on purpose, or was it a crime of opportunity? Did the killer follow her? Determine *Wheredunit*.

What is the means of murder? Does the deceased appear to have succumbed to an accident or to natural causes? Francine could have drowned in a ditch. Water-filled canals line the U-pick rows. But do I want it to look like an accident, or right away be identified as a homicide? She can fall into a silo and suffocate. Again, was it accidental or was she pushed? What would make her climb up there in the first place?

Or she could be run over by a tractor. Farms present lots of hazards. But if the murder involves an equipment accident, it'll have to involve someone who knows how to operate the machinery. You don't want to point the finger at a particular suspect like the farmer, because it's too obvious. Maybe give one of the other characters a secret history of working on a farm or of selling agricultural equipment.

In other words, what kind of specialized knowledge does the killer need? If a weapon is used, who has the means to obtain it and the experience to use it? Consider your means of murder very carefully when making these decisions so your story will be plausible.

In *Permed to Death*, I knew the victim would be Marla's crotchety customer, who would die in the shampoo chair while getting a perm. How would the woman be killed? Poison in her coffee creamer. Who had access to the special jar of powdered creamer Marla kept just for Mrs. Kravitz? The salon staff, other customers, and anyone who'd entered through the back door accidentally—or not—left open by the janitorial staff the night before. Since Marla was alone with Mrs. Kravitz and gave her the cup of coffee that led to her demise, Marla becomes the prime suspect. But if Marla didn't do it, who did?

The killer had to be someone with knowledge of the poison, the means to obtain it, and the opportunity to add the substance to the creamer jar.

If you're using poison, is it fast-acting enough for your purpose, or do you need a slower, more insidious death? What are the particular symptoms? When would it have to be administered and how? Where would your killer obtain it? Is it traceable, or will the death appear to be due to natural causes?

Keep in mind that cozy readers don't like a lot of mess, and not only in terms of blood. So skip the gastrointestinal symptoms if you poison the victim. Get a substance that acts quickly with a minimum of distress, or one that weakens the person over time via multiple dosages, such as a poison given in the victim's tea every evening. Sometimes murder may be suspected but not proven. In this case, you have to find a motive. **Why** would the matriarch's niece, gardener, caretaker, or neighbor want her dead? We'll talk more about motives below.

When does it happen? Think about the time of death, and also why it didn't happen a week or a month ago. Why NOW? What change has occurred or is imminent that threatens the killer? Or what new opportunity has arisen for him to carry out his plan? There has to be a reason why the murder occurs during your story instead of at an earlier time.

How does the killer get away? Does he have blood on his clothes and a dubious explanation for how it got there? Are his shoes wet or the cuffs of his pants muddy? Is he able to blend back into a crowd? Will he establish an alibi? How does he act when he encounters the sleuth? Think in terms of means, motive, and opportunity. One technique that helps is to interview your murderer. Let him tell you how he did the deed. Save this confession to use later in your story.

Now let's throw a wrench into the works. What if it's a case of mistaken identity? The villain thought he had killed one person but he got a look-alike instead. How will he react upon seeing his intended victim alive and well? This leads to another set of problems. It means he wasn't able to see the victim's face before he killed her, or he'd have realized it was the wrong person. So again, we go back to *Howdunit*?

Once you figure out these details, you can determine how your amateur sleuth stumbles across the dead body. And this is when your story actually begins.

Does the crime have to be a murder?

You could get away with kidnapping, theft, or another apparent crime as long as you follow genre conventions. There must be a puzzle to solve, and children or pets cannot be harmed. You'll want engaging characters and a whodunit-type plot even if it involves a missing object or person instead of a murder.

The stakes have to be high enough for the sleuth so readers care about the outcome, but not so scary as to impart a sense of dread. Any hint of sexual abuse or child abduction may turn cozy readers off. It's a delicate balancing act, and the lines between subgenres may blend. Keep in mind that cozy readers want a delicious tingle over danger, not a growing sense of impending doom as in a suspense novel.

You may want to make it clear in your story blurb that this particular title does not contain a murder mystery, so readers won't wonder when the body will show up.

How can you avoid police involvement?

The amateur sleuth will have skills the police don't possess for their formal investigation. For example, my hairdresser sleuth is a good listener. She can coax people into talking about things they wouldn't reveal to the police. A detective might be intimidating, whereas a suspect may be more willing to talk to your average gal next-door.

Reader expectations in this genre allow for the sleuth to find multiple bodies and for the police to be busy elsewhere or focused on the wrong suspect. They'll usually warn off the sleuth not to interfere. The important thing is to give your protagonist a personal reason to get involved and skills that will help her acquire the information she needs.

Create the Suspects

Now it's time to develop your suspects. Consider who has the most to gain from the victim's death. Who knew the victim, had access to the murder scene, and might have a motive? Besides obvious characters such as relatives and colleagues, include the innocuous lawn cutter or devoted friend. Everyone acquainted with the victim becomes a potential murderer.

Draw a large circle in the center of a piece of paper and write your victim's name inside. Now make branches extending out in all directions. At the end of each branch, draw a smaller circle and write the name of a suspect inside.

Along the length of the branch, write in the possible motive for each suspect or another secret that makes him seem suspicious. Now interconnect the branches to form a web of deceit.

Remember, one of these people is the killer. Is it the one with the strongest motive? Or is it the person who seems the least likely to have done the deed? Assign everyone a secret, whether it's a benign one like paying for a relative's care in an old age home, or a hidden grudge that could be a motive for murder.

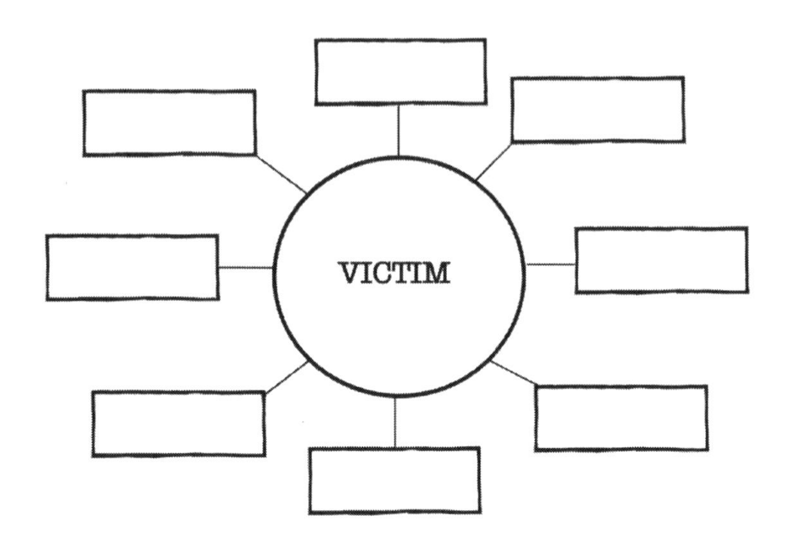

Here's an example from *Trimmed to Death* on how I develop my suspects. I'll do a brief blurb about each person first and their role in the story. Here's one of the judges from the bake-off contest at the farm's harvest festival:

Alton Paige, food critic, has a pudgy face and a rotund figure that reminds Marla of a dog. He's a bit of a philanderer. Alton extorts money from restaurant owners in return for a good rating. He resents the attention being given to upstart bloggers like Alyce Greene. Her blog is eroding his ratings and putting his job in jeopardy.

Oops, I have an Alton and an Alyce, one of the bake-off contestants. Watch out for similar names when creating your characters. I will change the judge's name to Carlton. In the next round, I fill in his secrets and start working on his relationships to other characters.

Carlton Paige, 44, food critic, has a pudgy face and a rotund figure that reminds Marla of a pug breed of dog. He's a philanderer whose sensual attitude in life appeals to women.

Carlton accepts gifts from restaurateurs. In return, he gives them a higher rating than warranted. The word to describe him would be smarmy. He speaks in a whiny nasal tone. He has a black lab and goes to the same vet as Marla. His wife, Sally, who accompanies him on his food jaunts, spends most of her spare time at the gym. She's always criticizing his lack of restraint in eating... and in other things. Secretly he has an inferiority complex, being the younger brother of three siblings. He strives for recognition. Food has been his means of consolation. He's worked his way up in journalism and aspires to be editor of the entertainment section. But that won't happen unless he gains readers. He resents the attention being given to upstart bloggers like Alyce Greene. Her blog is eroding his ratings and putting his job in jeopardy. What will he do to protect his reputation and his readership?

You see how each round adds another layer? These people will come alive when they walk onstage for the first time. I don't bother with long biographies. I'll see how they move and speak and act when I meet them on the page. For some of them, I may fill out a character development sheet. If you want to get a better handle on physical descriptions, search for images online at the royalty-free sites. These can give you more ideas for your characters. At this stage, what matters the most are their motives for murder.

Choose the Villain

Give your bad guy his own personal agenda. Why is this goal important to him? What is he doing to attain this objective? How do his actions affect the other characters?

- While you can hint at the villain's motives, the real reasons behind the murder aren't revealed until the final confrontation.
- Allow him to care about something to show his humanity. i.e. He may think nothing about bumping off the opposition, but he loves his dog.
- Have a "good" villain as well as a "bad" villain, i.e. an official who obstructs the heroine's efforts.

- The stronger the villain, the more stalwart the heroine must be to defeat him.
- The villain may have a twisted view of the universe. In other words, he doesn't see himself as being evil. His cause is just in his mind. This will only come to light during his confession at the end.
- Trick the reader now and then by having two villains. For example, one could be guilty of the first murder, and a different person could be guilty of the second one. Just when the heroine thinks she's safe because the bad guy is behind bars, she finds another clue that makes her realize there's a different killer out there. A secondary climactic scene occurs.

Here are some possible negative motivators for your murderer. Remember in a cozy, you want a personal motive for the crime. And while all suspects may seem guilty, the true motivating factor isn't revealed until the end.

Protect a secret, i.e. baby given up for adoption
Preserve reputation
Protection of a loved one
Clear an obstacle to a goal
Fear of discovery; Remove threat of exposure
Hidden identity
Greed
Jealousy/Envy
Love turned to Hate
Revenge
Having an affair
End source of blackmail
Filed for divorce/planning to leave spouse
Get rid of rival for loved one, promotion, or award
Covering up past or current misdeeds
Got fired or about to be fired

Cozy readers expect a certain type of story when they pick up a book in this genre. You don't want them grimacing in distaste or feeling your story is too painful for them. So make the villain as mean as you can within the limits of genre expectations. Also keep in mind what the bad guy is doing to avoid detection. How will he react when the sleuth's questions bring her too close to the truth? Will he attack or attempt to warn her off? Or threaten her in another manner? And while she attempts to guess who is targeting her, she won't get it right until the finale.

Why did the crime occur?

Newspapers can provide a wealth of inspiration for motives. All sorts of reasons can become fodder for the criminal mentality. Look at the headlines and see what dirt you can find. Office manager for a non-profit organization misuses funds? CEO lied about business trip? Teacher found with files of child porn? Affluent housewife is part of prostitution ring?

Clip out these articles and save them for when you're searching for secrets.

Examine the crime that is the basis for your story. *Whydunit*? Basically, you're dealing with individuals and their personal relationships. Was the basis of the crime greed to preserve an inheritance? Jealousy over a rival in a love affair? Or perhaps a cover-up for an illegal source of income?

Next you'll want to link your suspects to each other. Here's an example of how this works:

1. Alice is resentful of Dara, her boss, because Dara denied her a job promotion.
2. Dara is murdered. Did Alice kill her out of spite? Or does she have a stronger reason?
3. Alice is secretly having an affair with Brent, who is Dara's business partner. If Dara had found out, she would have fired Alice. This gives Alice a credible motive to eliminate Dara. Or maybe Dara had already discovered Alice's liaison with Brent.

4. But it also gives Brent a motive, because Dara thought Brent cared for *her*. If she found out about his affair with Alice, Dara might have revealed his corrupt dealings with one of their subsidiaries. He couldn't allow this to happen.
5. Brent, as Dara's successor, takes over her half of the company. Could greed have been another possible motive for him?
6. Michael, Dara's brother, is glad she's taken a family secret to the grave. He doesn't know that Dara confided in Brent. Had Dara threatened to reveal this secret before she died?

You get the idea. Here's another example from *Trimmed to Death* [Spoiler Alert]:

1. Marla and her friend, Tally, enter a bake-off contest at the harvest festival hosted by Kinsdale Farms. Tally heard about it from her friend, Becky Forest.
2. Becky Forest, a scientist, is a cookbook author and curator of the local history museum. She's also a contestant in the bake-off. Every time Becky has a new cookbook out, she's a guest on celebrity chef Raquel Hayes' TV show.
3. Raquel, a judge at the contest, has a mysterious past. Did she have an affair with the producer to get her show? Or is there a different secret she guards so diligently?
4. Francine Dodger, a food magazine editor and another contestant, may know what Raquel is hiding. Then again, while researching an article for an exposé, she might have uncovered something else that could make the farm owner lose his property.
5. Zach Kinsdale, who runs the family farm, hasn't told his siblings about the threat to their livelihood. Has Francine revealed to him what she'd discovered? Meanwhile, his sister Janet is married to Tony Winters, whose import company sponsored the bake-off event.

6. Tony is vice president of a gourmet food import business. His company's products are for sale in the farm's marketplace. He's worried about Alyce Greene, food blogger and bake-off contestant. Alyce knows something about his firm that could be troublesome.

There's more, but this is enough of an example. You can see how each person relates to another. If you haven't yet decided who the murderer is, you can pick the suspect with the strongest motive.

How many suspects are a good number?

I'd say six to eight suspects is workable, although I've read mysteries with only four people that kept me guessing. My stories tend to have a longer list. It really depends upon what evolves from your setting and the situation.

It's exciting when the puzzle pieces fit together as a whole, but this process may take a while. In the meantime, allow your subconscious to stew on these characters until Story Magic happens. The connections will pop into your brain. It's a joyful moment when this occurs. Have faith in the creative process, and it will happen to you.

Here's an example of a web of deceit from *Peril by Ponytail* [Spoiler Alert]:

PERIL BY PONYTAIL

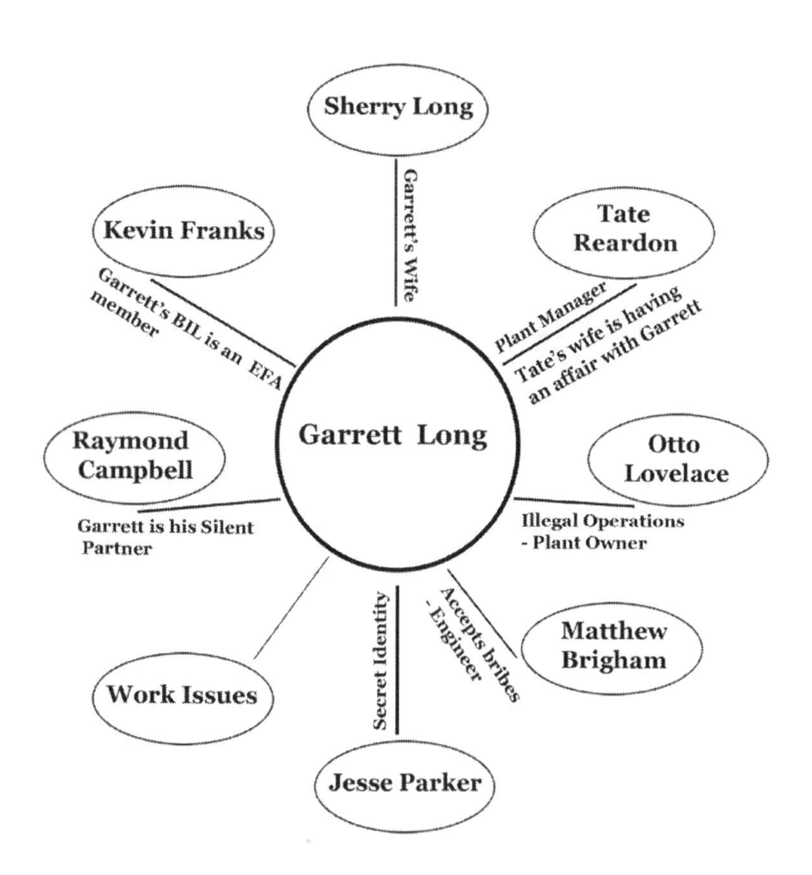

Writing Exercise

Sally Snoop and her friends attend a writers' conference where they meet keynote speaker Allison Highbrow. Allison makes a snide remark about the hot guy Sally met at the bar, implying his favors are nothing special. Later, Allison gives her speech, saying she's happy to be back in her home town where her writing career started. During the Vampire Ball that night, someone sends Allison a complimentary glass of wine. Her drinking habits are well known so when she keels over, people figure she's had one too many. It turns out she's dead. The drink was poisoned.

Now plot this story using the diagram above, keeping in mind the following points.

Who is the sleuth? What's at stake for her on a personal basis? Who are the suspects? What does each suspect have to hide? What is the villain's motive? Next do this for your own story.

Chapter Five – Heightening Suspense

Beyond the puzzle of the whodunit, various techniques exist that you can use to ratchet up the tension. You'll want to hook the reader in your first paragraph by hinting at a turning point or crisis in the main character's life. Start with action or dialogue to draw your reader into the story.

Once you've gained the reader's interest by creating likable characters, put those characters at risk. What's at stake if the sleuth fails? Her life? Her reputation? Her job? Another character's life she cares about?

Adding a time bomb raises suspense. This is a deadline beyond which disaster happens. False alarms can also heighten tension. The sleuth gets a scare but it's not real. The next time, she's slow to react but this is when it counts. Or isolate your characters. Being alone and out of range makes things scarier. It's worse if she left her cell phone in the car and has no way to summon aid.

Follow action sequences with reaction and reflection. Every action should garner a response from your character. It could be a decision on what she'll do next, or it could be an emotional response. Reflection on what's happened can lead to personal insight and character growth.

Give your character some down time. This is when you can have a romantic interlude, or have her review the suspects with her sidekick. It'll help vary the pacing. We've all seen movies with one chase scene after another, or battle sequences that seem as though they'll never end. The key is to vary the tempo. Let your readers draw a few breaths before socking it to them again.

But don't have too many slow periods, or your pacing will turn glacial. Move things along, either on the action plane or the emotional one.

Show, don't tell. Let us feel things along with the sleuth as they happen. You want to keep the story moving forward and not get dragged down by backstory, aimless conversation, or lengthy flashbacks. The tension should mount until the final confrontation. For this reason, it's often a good idea to throw in another dead body midway through your story. Or provide a plot twist that sends your sleuth in a new direction. This midpoint isn't for getting bogged down. It's a chance to raise the stakes and deepen the puzzle.

For faster pacing, use short paragraphs and steer clear of long expository passages. Work backstory into thoughts or dialogue in small snippets and only include what is necessary to the current crisis. Make sure each conversation has a purpose. Rambling dialogue kills the pacing same as expository writing.

As for chapter lengths, if they are too short, you risk annoying some readers. Nor do you want the chapters to go on forever. Mine used to be about fifteen pages until I started doing audiobooks. These came out to twenty minute segments in audio. Now my chapters are about ten pages each. This works for me, but you might mix up the lengths a bit more. Study the books you like to read and see how those authors do it.

When should the dead body show up?

You'll capture the reader's interest faster if you put the body up front. The alternate technique is to introduce all the suspects first. Make us wonder who is going to die. If you do it this way, you have to make the characters interesting enough to keep the reader turning pages. Perhaps you'll show us the sleuth in her normal life before the instigating factor arrives to draw her into the mystery. That would bc thc murder and her personal reason for getting involved. If you have an engaging author's voice, this technique can work well. But if you're in doubt, have the body show up sooner.

Foreshadowing

Foreshadowing allows the reader to anticipate bad things about to happen. This heightens tension, but it should be done using subtle techniques to avoid author intrusion. Remember to stay in your character's head.

Avoid out-of-body experiences, such as "If I knew what was going to happen, I'd never have walked through that door." Who has knowledge of the future? *The Author*, that's who. Certainly not your character, or she'd heed her own advice. Who else but the author is hovering in the air observing your heroine and pulling her strings? Same goes for these examples that are no-no's. Avoid this type of phrasing:

"I never dreamed that just around the corner, death waited in the wings." Who can see around this corner if not your viewpoint character? YOU, the author!

"Watching our favorite TV program instead of the news, we missed the story about a vandalized restaurant." If the characters missed the story, who saw it?

"I felt badly about the unknown victim, but it had nothing to do with me. Or so I thought." This person is speaking from the future looking back. If we're supposedly in his head, how is this possible?

"I couldn't possibly have been more wrong." Ditto to above.

"I was so intent on watching the doorway, I didn't see the tall figure slink around the corner." Then who did spot the tall figure? You got it—the author.

Your heroine places a perfume atomizer into her purse while thinking, "Before the day was done, I'd wish it had been a can of pepper spray instead." What happens later on? Only the author knows.

These are first person viewpoint, but the same principles apply to third person limited viewpoint. Your reader is inside that character's skin. She shouldn't be able to see/hear/feel beyond your heroine's sensory perceptions. By dropping hints about future events, you're losing immediacy. Avoid author intrusion by sticking to the present. Here's a better example:

The back of my neck prickled. I glanced around, but the woods remained quiet. Not even a bird chirped under the waning sun. Do you get a sense that something is wrong?

End of Chapter Hooks

Creating a hook at the end of a chapter encourages readers to turn the page to find out what happens next in your story. What works well are unexpected revelations, wherein an important plot point is offered or a secret exposed; cliffhanger situations in which your character is in physical danger; or a decision your character makes that affects story momentum. Also useful are promises of a sexual tryst, emotional aftermath of a love scene, arrival of an important secondary character, or a puzzling observation that leaves your reader wondering what it means.

Here are some examples from *Permed to Death* [Spoiler Alert]:

This was her chance to finally bury the mistake she'd made years ago. Gritting her teeth, she pulled onto the main road and headed east. (Important Decision)

"There's something you should know. *He* had every reason to want my mother dead." (Revelation from Suspect)

Her heart pounding against her ribs, she grabbed her purse and dashed out of her townhouse. Time was of the essence. If she was right, Bertha was destined to have company in her grave. (Character in Jeopardy)

"Todd Kravitz, the old lady's son. Don't you remember? He was the male model who posed with you for those sexy shots." (Secret Exposed)

Her heart heavy, she crawled into her car. Until this case was solved, she couldn't call anyone her friend. (Aftermath of Emotional Scene)

She allowed oblivion to sweep her into its comforting depths. (Physical Danger)

Decisions that have risky consequences can also be effective. For example, your heroine decides to visit her boyfriend's aunt against his wishes. She risks losing his affection but believes what she's doing is right. Suspense heightens as the reader waits to see if the hero misinterprets her action. Or have the hero make a dangerous choice that puts someone he cares about in jeopardy no matter what he does. What are the consequences either way? Moral quandaries always work. What if none of your hero's choices have a good outcome? End of chapter. Fans must keep reading to find out what happens next.

To summarize, here's a list of chapter endings that will spur your reader to keep the night light burning:

1. Decision
2. Danger
3. Revelation
4. Secondary character arrives
5. Emotional turning point
6. Sexual tension
7. Puzzle

Sprinkle the lucky seven judiciously into your story and hopefully one day you'll be the happy recipient of a fan letter that says: "I stayed up all night to finish your book. I couldn't put it down."

Writing Exercise

What's going to draw your readers into the start of your story? Will the body show up first, or will you introduce the suspects before the murder occurs? Why does your sleuth get involved in solving the crime? How do her actions put her in jeopardy? What's going to happen in the middle of your book to spur things forward?

Chapter Six – Solving the Puzzle

How do the suspects divert attention from the killer?

Give each of your suspects a secret, whether or not it relates to the victim. This will make your sleuth suspicious about what the other characters have to hide. Some of the secrets may be good ones, such as supporting a disabled aunt, or they might involve criminal activity that has nothing to do with the murder. Or the suspects might all have a motive for wanting an unlikeable character dead.

Don't forget to assign alibis, although not every character will have one. Some may be hesitant to reveal their whereabouts, while others may lie about where they were at the time of death. Still others may offer an alibi that contradicts something said by another suspect.

An additional ploy is to create two criminals, one who is the killer, and another person who has a personal vendetta for a different reason. This focuses the sleuth's attention on tracking down a seemingly guilty individual, while the actual villain emerges to pose the real threat in the final confrontation.

In other words, you don't want your road to go directly from Point A to Point B. Throw in as many curves as you can. If your synopsis changes during the course of the story as new plot twists make themselves known, that's a cause for celebration. Story Magic has come into play, and if you're surprised, your readers will be, too. You can always go back and rewrite the synopsis accordingly before presenting it to your editor.

How does the sleuth fit together the clues?

If you work backwards, you can figure out how each secret will be revealed to the sleuth. This will give you clues to plant throughout your story. How is the clue uncovered? It could be through omission, wherein something is missing from the scene. This may not be noticed by your sleuth right away, but later that item becomes significant. Or something could be out of place. If you disguise a clue by mingling it with other knickknacks, for example, the reader may not realize its presence until further along. Or you present the clue, then immediately distract the reader with a secondary character walking on scene or another exciting event. Having suspects rat on each other is another way of revealing information.

Think about the killer's viewpoint as you weave your storyline. Every move the sleuth makes brings her closer to the truth, and so the bad guy should make a counter move. Along the way, he might let slip an important clue. You can give him a false trail or a secret to make him appear guilty, and when that particular secret is revealed, it diminishes his apparent guilt. Or use red herrings involving other suspects to distract from the trail leading in his direction.

What is a Red Herring?

A red herring is a literary device that serves to distract readers from suspecting your real villain. Where did this phrase originate? In order to turn a herring into a kipper, the herring is cured in salt brine and then smoked for up to ten days. If enough brine is used, the fish turns a red, coppery color with a strong smell. Supposedly its meaning as a false trail originated with a news story by English journalist William Cobbett, c. 1805. He claimed that as a boy, he'd used a red herring to mislead hounds following a trail. This story served as a metaphor for the London press, which had published false news regarding Napoleon.

So how does this work for a writer? You allow readers to believe Suspect X may be guilty when it's really Suspect Y all along. It could be that you planned for Suspect X to be the killer but decided he was too obvious. Better to make him the red herring. Then while readers are following his trail along with the sleuth, you kill him off. The sleuth realizes he wasn't the murderer after all. Or, you can disclose a new fact that reveals his innocence and forces the sleuth to change direction.

You can focus attention on Suspect X by actions that make him seem guilty but that prove to have an explanation later on. Or maybe the police found evidence pointing to Suspect X while overlooking clues that lead to Suspect Y.

There aren't any hard and fast rules about planting a red herring. It has to spring logically from the story and make sense at the time. Remember to play fair and have several clues related to the real killer hidden along the way.

Plotting Structure

Once you've set the scene and know your characters, you are ready to begin plotting the story. Are you a Pantser or a Plotter, or a little bit of both? A plotter needs to outline the story ahead of time. This guide map gives a clear path to follow. Even if you're a plotter, the synopsis might change as Story Magic occurs. That's a sublime experience and can allow for surprises along the way. It's okay if you deviate from your path. You can go back later and rewrite or add in the extra scenes for your records.

A pantser flies by the seat of his pants, so to speak. He writes what comes and sees where the story takes him. The tale unravels as he writes. You could be a bit of both types in that you know certain elements of the plot but write as you go to fill in the details. Either way, here are some ideas to get you started:

1. Brainstorm plot points and put them on sticky notes on a plotting board.

2. Keep track of emotional turning points as well as plot twists.
3. Don't worry if gaps show in your planning. They'll fill in later.
4. Each scene should have a Purpose, Tension, Viewpoint, Action, Reaction, Decision.
5. Tools: Plotting Charts, Chapter Outlines, Software Programs, Timelines, Series Bible.

Think in terms of three acts. Act One involves the crime and introduction of the suspects. Show us the protagonist in her normal life. Then either introduce the suspects or have the murder occur. A turning point happens when the sleuth figuratively steps across the threshold from her daily routine and accepts the adventure. She makes it her mission to solve the crime.

In Act Two, the sleuth interviews the suspects and realizes they each have secrets. Potential motives are explored. Here you want to move the story forward in a logical manner. Who stands to gain from the victim's death?

Let's see how this works. In *Facials Can Be Fatal* [Spoiler Alert], one of the clients at Marla's day spa dies while getting a facial. Val, the victim, was a patron for a building preservation society. Their annual gala event is coming up, and Marla's stylists have been hired to do the models' hair at their designer fashion show. Marla has to salvage her reputation or risk losing this gig. Plus, she's applied for a position with a hair product company as an educator. Her opportunity to win this role might be jeopardized by the negative publicity. These factors give Marla the personal motivation to solve the crime.

First she considers the crime scene. Who had access to the treatment room besides the aesthetician? It could be another customer or perhaps a staff member. Had the murderer paid one of them to sabotage the item that led to the woman's death? If so, who else might be involved and why? Could it be one of Val's personal connections? Marla begins her investigation by interviewing the non-profit group's officers.

Deviating from this story, let's say the sleuth learns the victim—we'll call her Tina—had a boyfriend. When she interviews him, he states Tina was having problems at work with a colleague named Elizabeth. But Elizabeth claims the victim had been angry because she'd seen her assistant Dorothy sneaking out to lunch with the boyfriend. Who's telling the truth? The sleuth talks to Dorothy, who hints that our victim was having financial problems. The sleuth interviews Tina's landlord, who says... And so it continues. One suspects leads to another who leads to another. We're getting the idea that things aren't right with these people, but we're not quite sure what they're hiding.

The sleuth gains information through purposeful meetings such as interviews; casual encounters; or unexpected contacts. Your heroine might meet an informant who wants to get even with one of the suspects. Or she can trick a source through provocation or bluffing. Characters confide in her and offer gossip about other suspects. Suspects may even confess their own secrets as the story progresses. Often, the sleuth has a friend who can provide technical data. Tracing a paper trail is another means of discovering buried details. During this stage, the stakes rise, often with the appearance of another dead body.

Act Three is when the secrets are revealed, the number of suspects is narrowed, and the killer is exposed. It's like an onion. Each layer is peeled away until the inner core remains, and that's the murderer. A confrontation with the killer ensues. Readers of cozies expect this final battle. Make sure your heroine gets herself out of the fix and doesn't rely on acts of nature, a random accident, or the cops to rescue her. Give her the means or skills early in your story to make her actions believable.

Finally, I like to have a wrap scene or resolution where we see the sleuth back in her normal life. But something has changed. She's gained new insights from this experience. Here's where we learn how she has grown in her personal relationships over the course of her adventure.

To summarize the Three Act Structure:

1. Introduction of Suspects, Inciting Incident (i.e. dead body), Investigation, Conflicts build to First Turning Point
2. Secrets, Subplots, Complications, Rising Stakes, Second Turning Point
3. Clues unravel, Villain is exposed, Confrontation, Character Growth, Resolution

Should I write an outline or make up the story as I go?

Again, it depends if you're a plotter or a pantser. Once you know the characters, setting, and suspects, you can work on the storyline. The crime happens. Our sleuth has a personal reason to get involved. She begins by interviewing the suspects and learns they are all harboring secrets. Then it's a matter of the sleuth unveiling the clues and revealing everyone's hidden agendas. Each sequence should follow in a logical manner from the previous scenes.

If you're more of a pantser, you may know a few plot points, but you'll wing it as you go along. You might have more to fix at the end, but you can go back and trim out the overly lengthy passages or the scenes that don't go anywhere. You're also more likely to get stuck with this method if you don't plan ahead. But never fear; we'll talk about how to get your story moving again a bit later.

Either way, I'd suggest you write straight through until your first draft is finished. It helps to establish a daily or weekly page quota. Stick to this goal until you are done.

What types of questions must be resolved by the end of the story?

You have to tie up all **loose ends** pertaining to the mystery and identify the murderer along with his motive. Also let us know the consequences of his actions. Is he in jail? Was he killed in the final confrontation? What happens to him once he is caught? Justice must be served.

During your first round of revisions, it helps if you write down any questions that might arise in the reader's mind. Check off these points one-by-one as you answer each question further along in the story. Here is an example of the first few story questions from *Facials Can Be Fatal* [Spoiler Alert]:

What happened to Patty, the shampoo girl?
Who accessed Rosana's files and determined which products she used for Val?
Who changed Val's appointment time?
Is Marla's rival for the educator position involved?
Did Val confide any of her personal concerns to Rosana?
What is Sue Ellen hiding?
How far would Rodriguez go to get rid of Val?
Who was Val's former husband and where is he now?
Has Rosana been lying about her citizenship status?

What types of questions can be left unanswered from one book to the next?

Let's say your heroine is torn between two suitors in a romantic subplot. It's okay to carry this personal thread over to the next book, as long as the same issue doesn't drag on for too many volumes. Or your heroine might be having trouble committing to the guy she likes. Other unanswered questions might involve a secondary character with a secret or a missing family heirloom. Perhaps the thread left loose pertains to the heroine's background, something she needs to discover about herself. None of these relate to the current crime, which must be wrapped up by the end of each particular book.

These subplots add to the richness of the universe created as long as you resolve the subject further along in the series.

It's acceptable also to leave a hint pertaining to the next mystery. Some readers might complain about it, but others will be eager for your sequel.

Writing Exercise

How will your sleuth proceed once the murder occurs? What makes her want to solve the crime? Where will she start her investigation? Who does this lead her to next? Which other people might be involved? What action follows each interview? Describe the suspects. What motive does each one have to hide? Would one of them serve as a red herring? List three clues leading to the killer.

Chapter Seven – The Muddle in the Middle

While writing the mystery novel, you are plodding along during the first half of your book, and all of a sudden you come to a halt. Now what? It's too soon to start the revelations leading to the killer. You need more material to make your word count. If you're writing for a publisher, this might average 70,000 to 80,000 words. So what do you do? You face the blank white page and experience a sense of fear that your story will come up short. You've reached the dreaded Muddle in the Middle. But do not panic. Instead, read your synopsis over again and review your chapter-by-chapter outline. Haven't done them? Do so now. Reviewing what you've written will reveal plotting elements you might have forgotten or personal threads you can expand on. Here's what else you can do:

Raise the body count.

This is especially easy in a murder mystery. Throw in another dead body. Who is going to die and why? Who could have done it? How does this deepen the primary mystery? Could two different killers be involved? What if this victim was your prime suspect? Who does that leave? A whole new investigation will start based on who is dead, and it may throw your sleuth's earlier theories out the door. Now she has to go in another direction for answers.

Have an important character go missing.

If a character disappears midpoint in your story, that's going to disrupt everyone's plans. Is this person in jeopardy, or is he guilty of perpetrating the initial crime? Did another bad guy betray him? Or is this act staged, and the person isn't really missing at all? How do your other characters feel about this missing person? Was he loved or despised? What efforts are being made to find him? How are the police treating his disappearing act?

Introduce a new character who shows up unexpectedly.

Think about a secret baby, former boyfriend, or long-lost relative. What is this person's role in the mystery? How does his appearance change the investigation? Who else knew about him? This would be the time for that baby put up for adoption to come to light or the past husband no one knew about or the former colleague with a grudge. Or it could be someone who's heard about the case and wants to cash in somehow. Could this new arrival be a fraud? How does his presence affect the other characters?

Resurrect a character thought to be dead.

This is possible if a death was staged, meaning no body was ever found, or the corpse was not identifiable. Is it someone who'd been gone for years or whose alleged murder started the current investigation? What made this person decide to reappear now? Or, what is the clue that leads the sleuth to believe this guy isn't dead after all?

Steal a valuable object or return one.

Why was this item taken? Is it a clue to solving the mystery? Does it relate to another crime? Who took it and why? Is it meant to be a distraction from the murder investigation? Or was it part of the same crime all along? In the reverse, you could have a valuable object turn up, like a missing will or a more recent one that names a different heir.

Build on secrets and motives already present.

If you've laid the proper groundwork for your story, your characters have enough secrets, motives and hidden depths that you can explore as the story moves along. Write down each loose end as you review the high points and make sure you go down each trail until that thread is tied. Usually you'll find you have enough material already hiding among your pages. Snippets of suspicions can be plumped out until laid to rest. A secondary character who you've barely mentioned can become more significant. So give your people enough layers that peeling the onion takes the entire book.

***Surprises Happen* [Spoiler Alert]**

Something happens when you follow the principles above. Story Magic comes into play. Here are some of the surprises that popped out at me for *Trimmed to Death*. Hopefully the reader will be just as surprised and pleased by these unexpected plot twists.

- Francine's boyfriend belongs to an Egyptology cult. Could her proposed magazine exposé have been about him? Was he at the harvest festival the day she was killed?
- A resultant scene led me to research trees in religious rituals, such as the Acacia Nilotica. This tree, found in Egyptian mythology, contains Dimethyltryptamine, or DMT. It's the same compound used in shamanic rituals in the Amazon with a drink that induces psychedelic visions.

- The identity of Zach's wife.
- The true relationship between Alyce and Francine.
- A magazine photographer who works at Francine's publication was a surprise character. This made me wonder if there had been video footage of the harvest festival.
- Florida Squatter's Rights could provide a solution to one character's dilemma.

Each of these items led to a new scene. It was exciting for me to discover these angles and to figure them into the story. You can experience the same elation when you review what you've written and find hidden gems among your pages.

Writing Exercise

Go back and review your plotting notes. Is there an angle you've overlooked that you can use in the story? A loose thread you can expand on? A character you have neglected who might be important to the story? Will there be another murder? If so, who's the victim? How does this change the story direction? Or will there be an unexpected secondary character that shows up? How can you ramp up the excitement in the middle of your story?

Chapter Eight – Romance and Murder

Mystery fans enjoy a romantic subplot that is slow and subtle. The sex must be behind closed doors. Sexual tension is welcome and can be fun, but it's not an essential element. As for the heroine juggling multiple boyfriends, this gets old after a few installments. Have her make a decision. It doesn't have to be the right one, but it's less frustrating for readers than to keep stringing two suitors along.

Most of the fan mail I received early in my series involved the relationship between Marla and Dalton. Clearly, this factor was a big draw. Readers liked the slow burn of their developing love story. Marla chooses her guy and sticks with him despite the ups and downs of their relationship. The key is to have complications (i.e. internal conflicts) and for the couple to overcome the problems that keep them apart. Of course, once one complication is solved, you need to bring in another. Life is never smooth and always has conflicts.

Avoid turning your story into a romantic suspense tale. In this genre, the romance and the suspense element share equal billing. More than one viewpoint may be used, unlike the whodunit wherein readers stay within the sleuth's head. There are other differences between these genres. Foremost among them is that romantic suspense follows romance genre conventions while the classic cozy follows traditional mystery conventions.

Keep in mind that you are writing a murder mystery, and the romance takes second place to the puzzle of solving the crime. If you include a strong romantic subplot, your story may be termed a romantic mystery.

How to Blend Romance and Murder

In a series, you don't want to resolve the relationship by the end of book one. Build it step-by-step, advancing or retreating each stage per book.

Give your characters conflicts to keep them apart. The external conflict is your mystery. The internal conflict is the reason why the protagonists are afraid to commit to a relationship. Maybe your heroine was hurt by a former lover and fears getting burned again. Or she has a fierce need for independence because she has to prove herself worthy of respect. Why? What happened in her past to produce this need? Keep asking questions to deepen the motivation. Maybe your hero doesn't want a family because his own parents went through a bitter divorce. Secretly he feels he isn't worthy of being loved. Or maybe he suppresses his emotions and doesn't know how to give affection. Whatever the opposite sex character does seems to deepen or challenge this inner torment.

Your characters are immediately attracted to each other through physical chemistry. This pulls them together while the inner conflicts tear them apart. Yet the benefits of being a couple begin to outweigh the risks. As the characters become emotionally closer, they'll progress through the stages of intimacy.

Six Stages of Intimacy

1. Physical awareness: Your characters notice each other with heightened sensitivity. For example, the heroine is aware of the guy's physical attributes. She identifies his personal scent and feels a response in his presence. Show us this physical reaction and let us feel it with her.
2. Intrusion of thoughts: Your character begins thinking of this other person often. The love interest invades your character's mind.

3. Touching: First, it may be an arm around the shoulder, lifting a chin, touching an elbow. The couple comes closer until the desire to kiss is almost palpable. Have them lean in toward each other for a kiss and then interrupt it, so when they get to the next stage, it's highly anticipated. Use the five senses as much as possible to enhance the sexual tension.
4. Kissing
5. Touching in more intimate places
6. Coupling: In a cozy, these scenes are off the page. But if you're writing romantic suspense, you can include them. Here it's important to focus on the emotional reactions of your characters rather than the act itself. This is lovemaking, not just sex.

Throw a wrench into the relationship when all seems to be going well. His former spouse appears on the scene. Her off-again, on-again other boyfriend shows up. The heroine does something thoughtless and alienates the guy she likes. He feels pressured and backs off. Finally, they both change and compromise to resolve their differences. Let's see how this works.

***Bad Hair Day Mysteries* [Spoiler Alert]**

PERMED TO DEATH: Hairstylist Marla Shore meets Detective Dalton Vail. [girl meets boy]. While instantly attracted to each other, they share a mutual distrust. Marla is the prime suspect in her client's murder [external conflict]. Dalton is suspicious of her, and rightfully so. Marla hides a secret that gives her a motive. Meanwhile, Marla is suspicious of Dalton's interest because she thinks it's a pretense to interrogate her. At the story's end, he asks her for a date and she accepts [relationship moves forward].

HAIR RAISER: Marla meets Dalton's daughter [forward]. She dates a handsome accountant who earns her family's approval but may be a murder suspect [relationship moves backward]. Marla and Dalton share their First Kiss [forward].

MURDER BY MANICURE: Marla takes Dalton's daughter, Brianna, to dance class [forward]. Marla pretends to be her friend Arnie's fiancée so he can rid himself of an amorous old flame. They coax Dalton to date the woman instead. Marla gets jealous of Dalton when he pays the woman more attention [backward]. Marla earns his daughter's regard [forward].

BODY WAVE: Marla's ex-spouse, Stan, enters the picture when his third wife is murdered. Marla and Dalton work together to solve the case [forward]. Stan stirs up feelings Marla would rather forget. Dalton is jealous. Marla accuses him of wanting to pin the murder on Stan [backward].

HIGHLIGHTS TO HEAVEN: Marla and Dalton argue over his restrictive rules for Brianna, and Marla feels she has no place in his life if he won't listen to her advice [backward].

DIED BLONDE: Dalton acknowledges his need for Marla, and he proposes [forward].

DEAD ROOTS: Dalton meets Marla's extended family. He presents her with an engagement ring [forward].

PERISH BY PEDICURE: Marla meets the parents of Dalton's dead wife. Dalton takes their side [backward].

KILLER KNOTS: Marla meets Dalton's parents on a cruise. She and Dalton set a wedding date [forward].

SHEAR MURDER: Marla and Dalton tie the knot.

This last title is book ten, and I'm now up to book fifteen in my series. If your people get hitched, it doesn't mean their problems are over. Keep throwing roadblocks in their way. Life is never perfect. In reality, married couples still have conflicts as they learn to face life's challenges together. If you keep your sleuth single, make sure to motivate her choices to show why this path is right for her. Either way, keep things changing and evolving between your characters. It's this personal thread that compels readers to come back for more.

Writing Exercise

Will your sleuth have a love interest? If so, what is this person's role? What makes the pair attracted to each other? What keeps them apart? How will they overcome these issues? Is a third party involved? Will your sleuth make a choice at some point? Why is one suitor more right for her? Will any of your secondary characters get involved in a relationship?

Chapter Nine – The Grand Finale

As you near the finish line for your story, the tendency is to speed things up. You can't wait to be done and take a break. You're tired of the story and want it to end already. Or you're approaching your deadline and have to finish in a hurry. Yet this is when you need to slow down and let the finale unfold in exquisite detail.

The heroine's confrontation with the villain should reveal every heartbeat, every pulse-pounding moment of fear. You want time to slow so you can catch every nuance. Yes, the pacing must be quick, but you shouldn't cheat the reader out of emotional reactions, either during the scene or afterward. And the fight sequence, if there is one, shouldn't be rushed.

How about when the villain has been defeated? Consider having a Wrap Scene where your protagonist shares a quiet moment with her friends, love interest or family as they review recent events. Your sleuth comes to a realization about herself that prompts change. You always want to have this moment of character growth. A static protagonist who never changes will lose reader interest over time. Your heroine's relationships must evolve like in reality.

This last chapter is where you should tie up any remaining loose ends and perhaps frame the story with the same people or setting as the opening sequence. Putting some distance between yourself and the work will help you gain perspective. Go back after two weeks, if you have that luxury, and read the story again. Make sure you've resolved any questions about the crime.

When you reach the finale, flesh out any spots that are sparse and be sure you've covered all the bases. Your finale will dictate what impression readers take away when they close the book. For a series, you may want to insert a hint about the next story. A line or two will do, but it leaves an open thread for readers to pursue in the next installment. Just make sure this particular mystery is completely solved so your reader closes the book with a sense of satisfaction.

A Word on Revisions

Some writers like to revise what they've written before starting the new work for the day. This cuts down on later revisions. It's fine to use this method as long as you don't get bogged down making every word perfect. If you choose to write the rough draft straight through without another glance, you'll need a second pass through the manuscript for line editing. A third round may be necessary as you read through for continuity.

Watch for repetitions where you repeat information already given. It's easy to lose track of what your characters have said in earlier conversations. Keeping a chapter-by-chapter outline can help in this regard.

This is your chance to tighten sentence structure and pacing. Watch for scenes that need expanding or cutting, emotional reactions that are absent, inappropriate responses by your characters, or TSTL moments as mentioned earlier.

Does your dialogue sound natural or stilted? Do your characters all sound the same, or do they have different inflections? Is it clear who is speaking during conversational passages? In case your book goes into audio, give an indication of each person's voice quality. Is their speech clear, raspy, breathy, high-pitched, or whiny? Do they speak with an accent? Sprinkle in foreign words judiciously. Too many pronunciation barriers can annoy readers.

Do your descriptions contain enough sensory details?

Are you adequately conveying a sense of place? Are we noting these details from your sleuth's viewpoint?

If you have paragraphs that are lengthy, break them up. It's easier on the reader's eye to have more white space. Also, look for "laundry lists" of items that could be condensed. For example, "He cut the grass, tended to the weeds, watered the new sod, trimmed the hedges, raked the dead leaves, and stuffed the debris into a trash bag." You can summarize all this by saying "He did the yard work." Too many details can make the story drag.

Read through your book until you can't find anything else to fix. You can also try self-editing software to help point out problems such as repeated words, redundancies, or clichés.

If you want more feedback, consider entering a writing contest that provides comments along with the scores. Or attend conferences that offer manuscript critiques. Get involved in the writing community so you can learn about these opportunities. You should already be participating in a critique group, but now you need eyes on your entire work.

Once you've finished polishing the book to the best of your ability, you can send it to a freelance editor if you are self-publishing. Don't think you can skip this step. Even the most experienced authors need an objective look at their work.

Likely you'll need a developmental editor, who addresses overall story structure, pacing, and other important factors. A copy editor may be necessary, too. This person checks grammar, punctuation, proper names, and such. If you have a publisher, this is the time to submit the work to your editor or agent.

When you get the professional edits back, you'll undergo another round or two of revisions. When these are done, it's time to send the book to your beta readers, if you use them. This tier may involve fellow authors or enthusiastic fans who've had some experience in proofreading. They can offer valuable comments from a reader's point of view.

Finally, your work is ready for final submission. Send it back to your publishing house or to your formatter to put the book into production.

Read through your advance reading copies when you get them. Inevitably you'll find things that need fixing, either errors that got past you earlier or conversion problems, like misplaced lines or missing italics.

After you give final approval, you can heave a sigh of relief. The book is finished. Or is it? Doubtless you'll hear from readers down the road—sometimes years later—that you misspelled a word or made some other mistake. Nobody's perfect. No matter how many editing and proofreading rounds you and your editors complete, errors will still get past you.

Do the best you can and launch your baby out into the world.

Chapter Ten – Series Continuity

When you're writing a mystery series, considerations arise that do not occur in a single-title book. You have the same main characters in each installment. These are different from spin-offs that have a different set of protagonists for each story but utilize the same setting, family ties, or theme. In a mystery series, the background setting remains the same, unless your protagonist is a globe-trotter or goes away for a weekend jaunt. Here are some pointers to avoid pitfalls. We may have discussed a few of these items earlier, in which case consider this a reminder.

1. Give your sleuth personal motives for solving each mystery. This engages the reader's emotions so she'll care about what happens to your heroine.

2. Have your protagonist realize something new about herself by the end of each story. Character growth will bring more readers back to your series than if your sleuth never changes. Remember, characters compel readers, not crimes alone.

3. Spin a thread that continues throughout the series. In my stories, Marla falls for Detective Dalton Vail, but their budding relationship navigates a rocky road. He comes with a twelve-year-old daughter and has trouble letting go of his dead wife's memory. Marla

comes with an aversion to having children due to a tragedy in her past. Before they can share a future together, these two people have to surmount their problems and move forward.

In terms of subplots, a romance is always popular. You could also devise an ongoing search for a missing heirloom, a problematic relationship with a grumpy boss, or a clingy relative. Or perhaps the heroine is searching for something from her own past that has eluded her. The idea is to make readers eager for the next installment in your sleuth's personal life.

4. Create a setting broad enough so new people can come to town. Readers of this genre expect dead bodies to pop up in each story. However, to make this plausible book after book, give your sleuth a job where contact with the public is commonplace. Or make the setting somewhere that tourists visit or business conferences might be held. Your locale should include multiple possibilities for the setting within a setting as discussed earlier.

5. Be wary of leaving the place that your readers have come to love. Too many forays out of Townsville will disappoint fans who want to revisit familiar locales. For variety, consider having your sleuth track a suspect out of town for a chapter or two. Or move the action for one book and then go back to home base for the next installments.

   I've done this every few titles. *Dead Roots* (#7) finds Marla and Dalton at a haunted resort for a family reunion on Thanksgiving weekend. In *Killer Knots* (#9), they go on a Caribbean cruise with a killer onboard. Then it's back to home base at Marla's salon until *Peril by Ponytail* (#12), when Marla and Dalton take a honeymoon to Arizona.

This change of scenery can give you a break from monotony along with your readers, but do it too often and fans will get annoyed. In the meantime, you can vary the setting within the setting. This can provide refreshing variation within the parameters of your familiar home town.

6. Create a recurrent cast of characters who follow your protagonist from book to book. Make them interesting enough so each can grow their own subplot. These characters become friends to your readers, who look forward to revisiting them in each story.

7. A newbie should be able to jump into any one of your stories without previous knowledge from your other books. Introduce backstory in dialogue or brief introspections to keep the action moving forward, while including only the details necessary to the current plot. Also fill in each recurrent character's role so new readers will catch on, but be wary of too much repetition. It's a delicate balancing act, because you don't want new readers to feel lost, and yet you don't want to bore steady fans with material they already know. When you get beta readers, try to have someone new to your series in addition to people familiar with your work.

8. Don't reveal the killer from previous stories. Hinting at secrets from your other books may entice new readers to buy your backlist titles, and you don't want to give away whodunit.

9. Make sure each book stands on its own with a mystery that goes full circle and has a satisfying conclusion.

10. Address the Aging Conundrum. How fast will you age your sleuth? Will there be a big time gap between stories, or will the next book take place within months of the last one? Keep track of these time jumps, or else your sleuth will end up being too old to go gallivanting around town when you reach book twenty in the series.

Chapter Eleven – Organizational Tools

How do you keep track of all the characters?

It's helpful to keep two files, one for the recurrent characters and another for the group of suspects in each story. Define their key personality traits and see if you can find pictures online at the royalty-free image sites to help you visualize them. Or use actors for your inspiration. Keep the cast of continuing characters updated with each installment, and transfer this file to your new folder when you start the next book. Your suspects should be in a separate file as these will change for each story.

How can you remember story details?

When I started out as a professional writer, we had no sophisticated software to help us organize our material. I developed a process that helped me visualize the plot. Today there are many software programs available that can help you do the same thing.

For my earlier books, I used a storyboard or plotting chart. To use this method, divide a large white poster board into twenty blocks, or however many chapters will appear in your novel. Then write down all the plot points that come to mind on sticky notes. Put these around the board in some sort of order. This gives you a general guideline for writing the synopsis.

When the book is finished, remove the sticky notes and write each scene in colored inks directly on the poster. For example, I used black ink for story progression. Red ink was to identify loose ends. When these points were tied up, I'd underline the questions on the poster so I could see at a glance that I'd answered each one. Green ink was for clues leading directly to the killer, and blue ink was for introducing a new character. Keeping track of dates was trickier. I'd write in the month, day of the week, and time of day on the storyboard.

If you prefer, you can keep similar files on your computer if you choose not to use a software program. Currently, I do a chapter-by-chapter outline that helps me with the story's timeline progression. I also write down what information is revealed in each scene so as to avoid repetition. Often I'll fill in these sections after I've written them.

Keep a Plotting Notebook

The Plotting Notebook aids you in keeping track of each title. You'll need a one-inch binder notebook with colored tab dividers for the following sections:

Characters
The Sleuth
Recurrent Characters
Suspects and Villain
Life Space of Protagonist
Interview with your Sleuth
Confession by the Killer
Photos and Biographies
Character Development Charts

Plot
Ideas for story elements
Items to include or to fix along the way
New plot twists

Critique group comments until you get to address them
Loose Ends – the questions and clues that must be answered by the end of the book.
Timelines for character ages and birthdays, children's school levels, family tree, days of the week for this particular story. A calendar might be helpful.
Proper Names of shops, restaurants, pets, vehicles driven, housing developments
Project Timeline: Date you started project; milestones; date draft finished
Deleted Scenes that you can use as bonus content

Synopsis
A typed, double-spaced narrative in present tense describing the story
Original and revised versions

Sequels
Synopsis of your sequel if you have one written
Notes on plot elements
Personal threads that will carry over from current story
Titles of next books in the series and story blurbs
Notes on recurrent characters and their roles in subsequent stories
Overall series character arc
Research for next book

Contacts
People who have helped you with research; beta readers; and any other people who've provided aid or inspiration that you might want to include in Acknowledgments
Queries sent to editors and agents
Submission dates and responses

Research
Notes taken when you interview experts or scout a locale

Copies of articles and photos relevant to your story
List of online resource links
Brochures, menus, tourist pamphlets, maps, and other relevant printed matter
Use clear sheet protectors to hold items you don't want to get damaged
Ideas for blog topics based on your research

Production
If you are self-publishing, add this tab. Here will go notes and receipts for formatters, cover designers, freelance editors, ISBN numbers, distributors/vendors, expenses versus royalty income

Promotion
Promotional Campaign for each title
Story blurbs, back cover copy, tag lines
Endorsements and Reviews
Book Trailer text, photo and music sources if you're doing it yourself
Copies of print materials, i.e. bookmarks, postcards, business cards
Swag ideas, i.e. door hangers, coasters, pens, note pads, magnets
Blog articles and virtual tour schedule
Appearances List for Online and In Person Events
Long and Short Biography
List of Bloggers/Reviewers and their responses to your queries
Niche marketing tips
Copies of receipts for marketing efforts
Promotion Countdown Checklist
Book Launch Party
Book Release announcement for your blog
Press Release
Reader Discussion Guide (optional)

Chapter Twelve – Special Considerations

After you begin writing in this genre and get a few books under your belt, you may encounter some of these problematic issues. They are outweighed by the hours of reading pleasure you'll bring your fans. I thought I'd mention them here so you go into this venture with your eyes open.

- Lack of Respect – You're writing in a lighthearted genre that aims at an audience of mostly women. Like romance writers, you may experience a lack of respect for your talent and hard work. You'll see this at some conferences that a lot of "serious" crime fiction authors attend or at some literary awards that never choose cozies. The term "Cutesies" has even been used to label these books based on their punny titles and cartoonish covers. Don't mind these people. You're serving a multitude of fans who are dedicated to the genre and who gobble these books like candy. Plus, the subgenre is broad enough to cover these beloved romps as well as stories that lean more toward traditional mysteries. Readers will choose their own cup of tea.
- Recurring Dead Bodies – This dilemma happened to Jessica Fletcher in the infamous Cabot Cove where the "Murder, She Wrote" TV series took place. It's absurd for one person to stumble across corpses on a regular basis, but so goes the genre. Readers suspend their disbelief and expect a body count. Cozies are fantasies

in a way, because of this factor and because the bad guy is always caught. No serious harm comes to the sleuth, and justice is served. Accept that these books have a fantasy element and you can enjoy them for the mischievous romp they are meant to be.

- Irreverence toward the Dead – Other authors may feel our lighthearted stories don't show proper respect to the dead. Just because these stories have humor doesn't mean the author regards a murder victim or their family with disrespect. One is sorrowful for the survivors of the deceased, but humor can still come into play in other ways. It can be situational or stem from the sleuth's humorous outlook on life, which often reflects the author's voice.
- An Amateur at Play – Yes, the amateur solves the crime. Again, we are dealing with a bit of fantasy here. How many of us, as an average Joe or Joanne, would really go out and put our lives at risk to track down criminals? Yet in a cozy, the amateur sleuth outwits the crook and the cops at the same time.
- Lack of Police Presence – Why aren't the police detectives solving the crime? Again, these are amateur sleuth mysteries, and cozy readers accept this genre convention. Either the cops are focused on the wrong guy, or they don't take the crime seriously. Perhaps your sleuth will team up with the homicide investigator so they solve the case together.
- Limited Point of View – These stories are told from first-person or limited third-person point of view. Thus the reader only knows what the sleuth does through her perspective. If you show the criminal's mind and we know who it is, it's not a whodunit.
- No Graphic Sex or Violence – Your sleuth can't be terribly hurt in her confrontation with the killer. We want to see her bounce back quickly to solve the next

mystery, but make sure you allow time for healing if she's injured.

- Language Restrictions – You can't have bad language, except where it's necessary to accurately portray a character. But be aware your audience wants "clean" reads. Think "Hallmark Movies and Mysteries" when writing your book. Or use word substitutes, like "frak" or "freakin'" for the F-bomb.
- Setting Confines – As an author, you might get tired of writing about the same place over and over again. Yet the reader loves to revisit the characters you've created and the settings that bring comfort. If you need a change of pace, set the story elsewhere from time-to-time, but not too often. After I wrote *Killer Knots*, my cruise ship mystery, I got this letter from a fan: "*Killer Knots* left me a little disappointed as there was no mention of being in a salon and no mention of Marla's dog, Spooks." This reader wanted stories set in the same locale, but as an author, I needed a change of pace. You could avoid this problem by having a series that changes locations but keeps the same recurrent cast that accompanies the sleuth. Or vary the setting within a setting enough to reward yourself with a fresh outlook.
- Pets as Characters – As evidenced by the reader comment above, pets play an important role in cozy mysteries. Readers love for your sleuth to have a cat or dog or other animal at home. But remember genre conventions and never kill off this beloved pet. Also address the pet's care. Have the sleuth come home and take her dog for a walk, refill his water dish or food bowl, and give him a fond scratch behind the ears. He can even act the part of sounding board for the protagonist if your sleuth talks to him.

How important is originality?

Originality matters in the sense that you have a new angle to offer readers. For example, culinary mysteries will always be popular, along with books set in mystery bookstores or crafting circles. If you can't come up with a new profession for your sleuth, then try a unique setting with a regional flavor. Perhaps no one has written a cupcake bakery series set in a small New England town. So the location can make your story different. Or offer a variation on a familiar theme. Instead of a bakery, maybe the heroine owns an artisan chocolate factory, and she sells her specialty fruit-infused chocolate bits to the baker.

Of course, your characters will always be original because they stem from your world view. You could also step outside the box to try something totally new and different. In this way, you can push the boundaries as long as you meet genre conventions with a puzzle to solve, intriguing characters, an interesting setting, and a likeable amateur sleuth.

Whichever approach you take, be prepared to explain why your series is unique. When you pitch your story, an editor might say, "We already have a talking cat series. What makes your idea different from what's already out there?"

Can serious issues be included in a cozy?

Certainly, serious social issues can be explored in cozy mysteries. But you have to add in reader expectations. There are certain understood taboos, such as rape, child abduction, or incest. Cozy readers expect an escape from reality, not a reminder of the horrors in the daily news. When they pick up a book with a humorous title and a distinctive cover design, they anticipate a certain type of story.

Your sleuth can have a dark background, where she'd been abused as a child, for example, or she's done something bad that she regrets. This may influence her current actions, and that's okay as long as she strives to better herself. She can have flaws, but she also has determination and wit that help her solve crimes. Past events may haunt her, but they've given her strength. And even though she has faults, her good qualities outweigh them.

Besides the topic and your main character's attitude, consider the tone. Think fun and flirty instead of solemn and sedate. You risk straying from the cozy genre if you get too serious. You can have elements of a cozy in a story that is more somber, but these books lean more toward traditional mysteries. The term "edgy cozies" has been suggested, but is this really what fans want? Most cozy readers would rather turn the last page with a smile than a frown.

So here's a guideline. Include whatever topic lights your fire, but keep the story within genre parameters, or you'll risk alienating your readers.

What about paranormal elements?

Some readers enjoy stories with witches, ghosts, spirit dogs, or sleuths who talk to the dead. These can spice up a series with an added twist. But be careful to keep the focus of each story on the mystery. If you steer too far afield of the whodunit that's central to the story, you risk losing your mystery fans. The sleuth should be the one who solves the crime, albeit with clues handed to her or hinted at by her paranormal companions. But get too heavily involved in this otherworldly aspect, and you're steering toward another genre. Keep the mystery central.

When should a series end?

A series can end in several ways. It may not be the author's choice. In this case, your option book isn't picked up by your publishing house. You are orphaned when your editor leaves. The publisher cancels its mystery imprint. Or you receive an offer that is less advantageous so you turn it down. Here you have a choice of either self-publishing your sequels, finding a small press that will take on your series, or writing something totally new.

As a writer, you might experience burn-out. You're tired of writing about the same characters in the same setting and have run out of ideas or issues to explore. Or, you can't stand another minute on social media and are tired of the constant merry-go-round of marketing. In this case, it may be time to take a break or to write the book of your heart. Forget about the market. Write a story that brings you joy. It may rekindle your flame.

As a small business owner, the financial returns might not be as good as expected. Your writing budget may be in a negative balance. How long can you keep shelling out money when the returns don't warrant it? Should you write more books in this series or try something new instead? Or give up writing entirely?

These are tough decisions that only you can make. It's painful to end a series. You've been living with these people for so long that they've become imaginary friends. And it's even more difficult to start all over with a new setting and characters. The good thing is that you can always come back later and write another series episode, or toss in a piece of short fiction now and then. So unless you're retiring, a goodbye may remain open-ended.

These issues aside, writing cozies is a gratifying experience. You are providing your readers with hours of escape. Feedback from fans is what makes it all worthwhile. Just knowing you've brightened someone's day will inspire and encourage you to keep writing.

Chapter Thirteen – Keeping a Series Fresh

Once you've written several books in your mystery series, it gets harder to come up with new and interesting material. The story has to engage your senses as a writer if you care to entice readers. You'll want to avoid repetition such as means of murder and motives. And you need to vary the locales without going too far afield. Probably the most important element is to grow your characters. Let's look at what you can do to bring excitement to each story in a long-term series.

1. Vary the setting within the setting. My Bad Hair Day series is set in fictional Palm Haven, Florida. But each story has its own milieu. *Permed to Death* introduces hairstylist sleuth Marla Shore in her hair salon when a grumpy client dies in the shampoo chair. Subsequent stories involve a seaside estate, sports club, wealthy family's mansion, beauty trade show, wedding party, and day spa.

   As for varying the locale, Marla has taken day trips to interview suspects at Cassadaga, Tarpon Springs, Delray Beach, and other Florida environs. For a change of pace, she's gone on a Caribbean cruise and taken a dude ranch honeymoon to Arizona. For me, those stories are particular fun, but I can't do them too often. Readers like to return to the familiar home town they've come to love. To avoid boredom, you have to change the setting for each mystery enough to keep it interesting for you and your readers.

2. Avoid using the same murder method twice. Have you poisoned a victim already with a plant potion? Use snake venom next time. Or try shooting, hanging, stabbing, bashing on the head, pushing down the stairs, etc. Avoid repetition and be creative. Also vary the villain's motives. You don't want two stories in a row where a jealous lover did the deed. Think of your negative motivators to provide variety.

3. Character growth is the key. Your protagonists should evolve like people do in real life. Who surrounds them in terms of family, friends, and colleagues? How do their relationships change in each story? What's the overall emotional journey for your main character? What new person can you add to spice things up? It could be a friend, an old flame, a secret baby, a new boss, or a romantic interest. Keeping your main character static won't work. The protagonist must continually adapt and expand her goals while letting insights guide her actions.

4. Include a research or historical angle that excites you. In *Facials Can Be Fatal*, I used excerpts from my father's true life 1935 travel journal, which detailed his trip to Florida in simpler times. History plays a part in this story with tales of shipwrecks and pirates off the Florida coast. As a matter of interest, I published my dad's journal separately as *Florida Escape*.

   For *Trimmed to Death*, I've researched olive oil scams, olive groves, and olive lore. If you're thinking I must love olives, you are right. I enjoyed learning about this popular food item. Are olives a fruit or a vegetable? How do green olives differ from black olives? Is this food beneficial to your health? Why is the olive branch a symbol of peace? You can be sure this trivia will make its way into my blogs when the book debuts.

You can explore all sorts of eclectic topics for your stories. These tidbits of information may capture your interest, but they'll also provide something fresh for readers. Avoid info dumps, however, where you have long expository paragraphs with too much detail. Your research shouldn't show. It should enhance your story. Save the esoteric details for guest blog posts.

5. Sprinkle in local issues or social problems that concern you. In *Hair Brained*, one character tells Marla about the risks to children left in hot cars. This is a big issue in Florida where heatstroke is the leading cause of non-crash, vehicle-related deaths for children. Other topics I've touched upon include child drowning prevention, estate planning, biohazardous waste disposal, illegal migrant labor, and more. These subjects can provide added depth to your story, but do it in a way that suits your chosen genre.

6. Consider using some of the same techniques as in the middle of a book to liven things up. Kill off a secondary character (but not the love interest, or you'll anger readers like me). Use the secret baby trope. The hero had a child he didn't know about. Or a baby given up for adoption seeks her mother years later. Bring back an old flame or a school mate, or reveal an unknown branch of the family. Introduce a missing heirloom or an unclaimed inheritance. Or perhaps a relative has disappeared. These ideas could breathe new life into your series.

Chapter Fourteen – Writing the Smart Synopsis

Do you dread writing a synopsis? If so, get used to it, because this tool is essential to your career as a writer. Not only is a synopsis necessary for a book proposal, but the sales force at your publishing house may use it to design your cover or to plan marketing materials for your book.

A synopsis is a complete narrative of your story told in present tense. It should include essential plot points plus your character's emotional reactions. The synopsis can act as a writing guideline while not being so rigid that your story can't change. When you finish the actual writing portion, you can return to the original synopsis and revise it to suit the finished storyline.

So how should you proceed?

- Consider adding a tag line on your first page before the story begins. More on this below.
- Open with a hook.
- Use action verbs. Your story should be engaging as you convey it to the reader.
- Make sure the story flows in a logical manner from scene to scene. Present the crime, the suspects, and their secrets. Then show how the sleuth uncovers their hidden agendas and unravels the clues.
- Avoid backstory. Stick to present tense and keep the story moving forward. Enter background events in small doses via dialogue or interspersed with action, and only if it applies to the current situation. Less is

better. And don't reveal too much up front. It's best to keep the reader guessing.

- Leave out minor characters, physical descriptions unless applicable to the storyline, and subplots unless critical to the resolution of the main plot.
- Avoid snippets of conversation, point-to-point description of your character's every move, jumping from one place to another without a transition, gratuitous sex, or threats on a character's life unless they evolve from the story.
- Include your character's emotional reactions.
- Stay in the protagonist's viewpoint as you would in the story.
- Show your character's internal struggle as well as her external conflict. What's inhibiting her from making a commitment to the hero? What is causing her to doubt her abilities?
- Tell us what's at stake for the heroine. What will happen if she fails?
- If it's the first book in a series, you might begin with a short profile of your sleuth.
- Explain the ending. This means you should tell *whodunit* and *whydunit* to show your agent or editor that you know how to bring the story to a logical conclusion.
- What life lesson will your protagonist learn in this story?

Example from *Facials Can Be Fatal* [Spoiler Alert]:

Salon owner Marla Vail's new day spa hits a snag when a client dies during a facial.

Screams emanating from next door draw salon owner Marla Vail's attention. She rushes into the adjacent day spa to see a crowd gathered in front of a treatment room. It appears

Rosana Hernandez, an aesthetician, was doing a facial on her first morning client. She'd put on the woman's chemical mask and left the room for ten minutes. Upon her return, Valerie Weston was dead.

Since the receptionist had enough presence of mind to call 911, Marla enters the treatment room to see if CPR will help. It's too late. The woman has no pulse, and her skin is clammy. A greenish cream mask clings to her face.

The police arrive, along with Marla's husband, Detective Dalton Vail. He takes charge of the scene and questions Rosana. The tearful beautician claims Val had been a long-time customer, and the only known problem she had was a latex allergy. Rosana was careful not to use latex gloves in her presence.

Marla, owner of the spa plus the salon, is upset about the negative publicity this incident will generate. She has applied to become an educator for Luxor Products, whom she'd worked for once at a beauty trade show. A smear on her reputation would be detrimental to her chances of winning the position. But she's also concerned about Rosana and proving the aesthetician wasn't at fault.

Lab tests confirm liquid latex had been added to Val's facial mask cream. Val died from anaphylactic shock. Rosana denies her involvement, and Marla believes her. So who else had access to the room, and why would someone target Val?

In this opening, we see the setup for the crime and what's at stake for Marla. She has an additional problem, which we'll learn about when she realizes why Val's name sounds familiar. In order to salvage her reputation and that of poor Rosana, Marla jumps on the case. Next, she'll consider who might have had a reason to harm the victim. This leads her to the suspects. Each person will be introduced in the synopsis as in the story. They all have secrets, which Marla will uncover as she continues her investigation. My double-spaced synopsis for this story runs twelve pages.

The One Page Synopsis

Your publisher requests a one-page synopsis. How do you condense an entire story into a single page? Here's what I do for my cozy mysteries. We'll use *Shear Murder* [Spoiler Alert] as an example. Let's start with a tag line that sums up the plot.

A wedding turns deadly when hairstylist Marla Shore discovers a dead body under the cake table.

The Setup

This initial paragraph presents the setup for the story. Here is where you present your opening hook.

Hairstylist Marla Shore is playing bridesmaid at her friend Jill's wedding when she discovers the bride's sister stabbed to death under the cake table. Torrie had plenty of people who might have wanted her dead, including her own sister who threatened her just before the ceremony.

The Personal Motive

Why does your sleuth get involved? Show us what compels her to solve the crime and what the stakes might be if she fails.

At Jill's request, Marla agrees to help solve the case. With her own wedding four weeks away, her salon expanding into day spa services, and her relatives bickering over nuptial details, she has enough to do. But when Jill is arrested for Torrie's murder, Marla has no choice except to unmask the killer.

The Suspects

Give a brief profile of the suspects along with their possible motives. Avoid mention of secondary characters that don't play a major role in the story.

Jill and Torrie owned a piece of commercial property together. Their cousin Kevin, a Realtor, has been trying to find them a new tenant. Meanwhile, Jill's uncle Eddy, a shady attorney, has been urging them to sell. Now Torrie's husband, Scott, will inherit his wife's share. Scott has another motive besides greed. Torrie had announced her plan to leave him for another man, Griff Beasley. Griff was Torrie's colleague at the magazine where she worked as well as the photographer at Jill's wedding. Griff implicates Hally, another coworker. Hally and Torrie were competing for a promotion. Then [Suspect X] turns up dead.

The Big Reveal

The final paragraph is where the clues lead to the killer. If possible, include what insight the protagonist has gained. This last is important for emotional resonance so readers will be eager for the sequel to see what happens next to your heroine.

It appears Suspect Y did [Evil Deed]. While snooping into his background, Torrie learned that Suspect A helped him [Do Something Bad]. Suspect A murdered Torrie because she found out about [An Illegal Activity], and then Suspect X because she'd discovered [fill in blank]. Marla reveals the killer and is free to enjoy her own wedding ceremony.

No, I'm not going to tell you who the killer is in *Shear Murder*. You'll have to read the book to find out. But this gives you an idea of how to write a one-page synopsis. Naturally, for my editor, I've filled in these blanks, and you need to do the same in your synopsis as well.

Story Blurbs, Tag Lines, and Log Lines

The story blurb is different from a synopsis as described above. A blurb acts as your back cover copy and as the book's description at various online vendors. This consists of 100-

250 words or one to three paragraphs highlighting the essence of your story along with metadata-rich keywords. You'll need a short blurb and a long blurb for different purposes.

The **Long Blurb** serves as the back cover copy for a hardcover edition. You can also use it as the book's description on your website and at various online book vendors. Here is an example from *Shear Murder*:

Weddings always make Marla Shore shed a tear of joy, especially when she attends her friend Jill's affair as a member of the bridal party. Marla's own nuptials are weeks away, and she's been busy juggling bickering relatives, building a new house with her fiancé, and expanding her hair salon.

The South Florida stylist is following her To-Do list just fine until an unexpected event unravels her carefully laid plans. At Jill's wedding reception, Marla discovers the matron of honor—Jill's sister Torrie—dead under the cake table, a knife embedded in her chest.

Unfortunately, Jill has a strong motive for murder. She and Torrie co-owned a piece of commercial property, and they'd disagreed on whether to sell or lease the land. Now with Torrie out of the way, Jill's decision can rule. Or can it? Her relatives may have some say on who gets control, meaning Jill can't trust any of them.

Torrie knew secrets about her colleagues, too, things they wouldn't want revealed. But when Marla learns one of those secrets involves Jill's past, she wonders if her friend is truly innocent. She'd better untangle the snarl of suspects and iron out the clues before the killer highlights her as the next victim.

Shear Murder is a fast-paced humorous mystery that will have you rooting for Marla to walk down the aisle with her groom before another disaster befalls her.

The **Short Blurb** can be used for marketing purposes, i.e. for a blog tour, on your website, and anywhere else that requires a book description. For my indie published books, I prefer this shorter blurb for the trade paperback back cover along with some review quotes. Here is the one for *Shear Murder*:

Weddings always make Marla Shore shed a tear of joy, and she's elated to attend her friend Jill's reception. Marla's own nuptials are weeks away, and she's busy following her frenetic to-do list. Her plans go awry when she discovers Jill's matron of honor dead under the cake table, a knife embedded in her chest. Lots of folks aren't sorry to see Torrie go, especially since the bride's sister knew their deepest secrets. But when suspicion falls upon Jill, Marla wonders if her dear friend is truly innocent. She'd better untangle the snarl of suspects and iron out the clues before the killer highlights her as the next victim.

Keywords are search-engine friendly terms that readers might use to find your book. For example, "cozy mystery" or "amateur sleuth" or "murder mystery" are popular for this genre. Mention your subcategory if it applies, such as culinary, crafting, or animal mysteries. Get even more specific and add things like "ghosts" or "psychic" if your story has these features. Put different terms into the search feature at Amazon and see what pops up. Look at the categories in the left sidebar. Amazon bestseller lists can also give you clues on what phrases to use. For help on Keywords, go to https://kdp.amazon.com/en_US/help/topic/G201276790.

Have a ***tag line*** ready to go if a reader asks "What is your story about?" This one-liner hook can also serve as a quick "elevator pitch" if you suddenly find yourself with an editor in the elevator at a conference or seated next to an agent at the lunch table. The ***log line*** is similar but longer and can consist of two or three sentences. Here are examples from *Shear Murder*:

Tag Line: A wedding turns deadly when hairstylist Marla Shore discovers a dead body under the cake table. (Also serves as your "elevator pitch.")

Tag Line with Keywords: A wedding turns deadly when hairstylist Marla Shore discovers a dead body under the cake table in this killer cozy mystery. (This can go in bolded letters above the book's description at Amazon.)

Log Line: Who knew weddings could be murder? Hairstylist Marla Shore is weeks away from becoming a bride herself when she walks down the aisle as a bridesmaid at her friend Jill's ceremony. Things take a turn for the worse when the matron of honor ends up dead, the cake knife in her chest. Now what will they use to cut the cake? (Use this one for marketing purposes when you want a few more lines to hook reader interest.)

Some sites will limit your blurb word count, so it helps to have these summaries in different lengths. Some authors use the tag line or log line terms interchangeably. Either way, these are catchy sentences and short paragraphs that encapsulate your story. There are no solid rules on where and how to use them. It depends on the site and the requirements.

If you need assistance in writing a blurb, check out these resources:

Blurb Writer at http://www.blurbwriter.com/
Blurb Bitch at http://www.blurbbitch.com/
The Killian Group at http://thekilliongroupinc.com/

Chapter Fifteen – Mystery Movies

In addition to classics like Sherlock Holmes and Agatha Christie, here are some of my favorite films in the mystery genre or movies involving writers. Many of these are good examples of cozy mysteries. There are many more out there than I've listed, but these are the keepers in my home library. Watch them and look for the clues, the setting within a setting, the quirky characters, and the other elements we've discussed.

Films and TV Movies

American Dreamer with JoBeth Williams and Tom Conti.
This classic tale of intrigue is one of my favorites. A romance novelist wins a contest and a trip to Paris. En route to the awards luncheon, she's in an accident and suffers a head injury. She wakes up believing herself to be the heroine in her favorite books. A spy caper follows that's all too real, as she teams up with the author's handsome son who thinks she's a nutcase. That is, until someone tries to kill them.

Drowning Mona with Danny DeVito and Bette Midler.
This funny whodunit in a small town has a cast of wacky characters. Classic example of a cozy.

Gosford Park with Helen Mirren and Jeremy Northam.
This is an English drawing room mystery that takes place at a country estate. Aristocrats and servants alike have secrets that

slowly unravel during a hunting party weekend. Albeit a bit slow-paced, this film requires repeat viewings to catch the nuances.

Her Alibi with Tom Selleck and Paulina Portzkova.
This hilarious escapade finds mystery novelist Phil Blackwood falling for a suspected murderess while he searches for inspiration to unlock his writer's block. Did the mysterious and beautiful foreigner have a hand in the victim's death? If so, was he foolish to vouch for her alibi and bring her home? And are the accidents that occur after her arrival truly accidents, or is Phil next in line for his guest's lethal hijinks?

Manhattan Murder Mystery with Woody Allen and Diane Keaton.
A Manhattan housewife thinks her next-door neighbor is a murderer. She enlists her friends to search for clues. Are her suspicions real, or is she imagining things?

Murder 101 with Pierce Brosnan.
English professor Charles Lattimore assigns his class to plan the perfect murder as a literary exercise. When he's framed for a woman's death, he has to find the killer before the detective on the case finds him. Will his students help him solve a real murder, or is one of them guilty?

Murder By The Book with Robert Hays.
A mystery novelist thinks he's hallucinating when his hero appears in front of him and talks back. He's been thinking of changing to a new series and scrapping the sleuth, but now he needs the fellow's help to solve a real murder.

Murder On The Orient Express, a remake of the classic Agatha Christie tale, with Johnny Depp, Judi Dench, and Penelope Cruz in an all-star cast. While not an ideal representation of the book, this film is worth viewing for the scenery and to see the actors in their roles.

My Cousin Vinny with Joe Pesci, Ralph Macchio, Marisa Tomei, and Fred Gwynne.
In this funny courtroom drama, a New York lawyer on his first case defends two men in Alabama who are mistakenly accused of murder. Watch for clues in this hilarious mystery.

The Boy Next Door with Dina Meyer and Cory Monteith.
A romance writer goes on a retreat to a small town to seek inspiration for her next story. When her neighbor is found dead, the chief of police suspects her. Even when her place is ransacked and someone tries to run her off the road, he discounts her theories and refuses to look into the incidents. It's up to our heroine to prove her innocence and uncover the killer before his next attack turns fatal.

True Memoirs of an International Assassin with Kevin James.
This Netflix original movie features a novelist whose fictional escapades become real in a comedic action-adventure tale. After a publisher changes his novel about the experiences of a global assassin from fiction to non-fiction, the author is abducted and ordered to kill a foreign president. Each denial of his true identity gets him deeper into trouble. The only way to survive is to assume the persona of his fictional character.

TV Series

The Brokenwood Mysteries with Neill Rea and Fern Sutherland.
Detective Senior Sergeant Mike Shepherd and Detective Constable Kristin Sims solve mysteries in New Zealand involving a limited number of suspects, most of whom know each other, in a distinct setting and with a definite sense of humor. Although this series is a police procedural, the emphasis is on interpersonal relationships among the characters and on personal motives rather than forensics. Each

episode is a perfect example of a cozy mystery despite the lack of an amateur sleuth.

Miss Fisher's Murder Mysteries with Essie Davis and Nathan Page.
The Honorable Miss Phryne Fisher solves crimes in 1929 Melbourne, Australia. Essie Davis plays the lead while Nathan Page plays her romantic interest, Detective Inspector Jack Robinson. Miss Fisher's spectacular outfits, along with her feisty independent nature, bring a flashy elegance to the genre.

Watch the Hallmark Movies and Mysteries Channel for cozy series on the small screen. http://www.hallmarkmoviesand mysteries.com/

Chapter Sixteen – Marketing Tips

Publishing Choices

Writers today can choose to submit their work to traditional publishers or small press, or they can take the indie publishing route. If you are seeking a publisher, I suggest you review the Mystery Writers of America list of approved publishing houses at http://mysterywriters.org/.

For a traditional publisher, you may need to find an agent. How can you do this? Sign up at writers' conferences for editor/agent appointments. If your group runs a local event, volunteer for the editor/agent committee. Enter writing contests where agents are the final judges. Note the acknowledgments to agents in books by favorite authors in your genre. Search the *Guide to Literary Agents* or *Writer's Market* at your local library.

Follow agents on Twitter. Look for the hashtag #MSWL (manuscript wish list). You can get more specific for a particular genre (i.e. #MSWL Mystery). Also check out #Pitchmas, #AdPit, #Pit2Pub, #PitMad, #AgentsDay, #Carinapitch, #PitMatch for online pitches. Use #AskAgent if you want to find agents who might be interested your story.

Follow blogs by well-known agents and publishing industry professionals. You'll learn who these people are by getting involved in the writing community.

The same goes for editors. Enter writing contests where editors are the final judges. Make a pitch appointment at a writers' conference. Check online for the publishing house's submission guidelines before you approach them.

Have a synopsis ready to go. You may need a short or long one depending on publisher requirements. Even if you are self-publishing, your cover artist may request a synopsis. There are blurb writers who can help you do the back cover copy, and these people might need your story summary as well.

Be prepared to pitch your novel as part of a series. Have a catchy series title. Describe what makes your sleuth unique and what motivates her. Write blurbs for the next two sequels. You're presenting this as a package to a publishing house. In a query letter, state the word count and genre, the title of your work, a brief story blurb, your credentials as a writer, and your series concept. If the editor is interested, you can send along a sheet with the series proposal.

Decide if you want your book in print and/or in ebook format. Would a digital first publisher be right for you? Do you want to see your book in physical bookstores, or will having it available via print-on-demand be enough? Do you hope for a hardcover library edition or a trade paperback? Think about these options while deciding where you want to submit your work.

Join your professional writing organizations and ask fellow authors how they like working for their house. Then prepare your pitch or query letter. Some houses ask for cover art suggestions and blurb copy. Don't assume they will do all the work for you. Whichever route you choose, you'll be doing your own marketing.

If you decide to go indie (i.e. self-publish your work), make sure your manuscript is as polished as it can be. Hire a developmental editor, do your final revisions, then have a copy editor and proofreader comb through the work. Get beta readers who are fans of your genre. Hire a cover designer and formatter to create a professional product unless you have skills in those areas.

You'll also have to decide if you will upload directly to online vendor sites or go through a third-party aggregator. It is not within the scope of this book to offer advice on self-publishing in detail. This information is widely available on various blogs and online forums.

If you'd like to be a hybrid author, publishing both with a traditional publisher and on your own, be careful to check your contracts to make sure you retain the rights to your characters and series. This is a good solution if you are more prolific than your publisher allows or if you want to publish short fiction in between your full-length books.

Author Branding

Whichever route you choose for your publishing career, consider your author brand. What message do you want to get across to readers about the type of books you write? This goes beyond individual titles or even series. If you're not sure of these qualities, take note of your reviews. What core elements do readers mention most about your work?

Create an author tag line. Use it on your website, in your email signature lines, and on your business cards. Here are some examples from other authors without mentioning names:

Romance Edged with Danger
Romance, with a Twist...of Mystery
Southern Mystery & Suspense
Mystery & Suspense with a Dash of Myth & Romance
Psychics, Serial Killers, and Snark
Smart. Funny. Murder.
Romance, Mystery, and Magic
Sexy, Suspenseful, & Seriously Funny

If you are indie publishing, having an engaging book cover is critical. What type of "look" do you want to convey? Study the cozy covers that catch your attention. Do you like cartoony covers or more realistic ones? Is this best done with photography or illustration? Do you like people on the cover, or scenes depicting the story? If you like people, do you prefer full-body images or waist-up only? How about a series logo?

Can you describe a particular scene you envision, or images that might work? It's good if you can suggest a few choices to your cover designer. If you have a traditional or small press publisher, you may be asked to fill out an art sheet. So either way, you need to know your preferences.

Placement of your author name, book title, fonts, and series logo should remain the same from cover-to-cover. So should the palette of colors. Don't go from pastels to bold shades. Stick with the same at-a-glance look that readers will recognize.

If you are self-publishing, consider what you want on the back of your trade paperback cover. A solid color or the front image bled in as background? Do you prefer to have a longer story blurb, or a short blurb plus some review quotes? And don't forget the spine. What should go there?

Make sure your print materials match your author brand. The same images and colors can populate your postcards, bookmarks, and business cards. Even your giveaways can include theme-related items.

Your social media sites should reflect your brand. Carry across your images, colors, and the overall tone of your work to the headers on your sites. Think beyond your books to your overall author image. You might change genres in the future, but likely your stories will retain the same core elements.

Reviews

Reviews are tough to get, especially for new authors. Ask your Facebook friends and newsletter subscribers if anyone is interested in reviewing your work. Before handing out a free copy, ask where they post their reviews. You don't want people just looking for a freebie.

Examine posts from other authors in your genre and see what sites they visit on their virtual book tours. Check the submission guidelines for these hosts and send out queries.

Have your book available in multiple formats. You can offer a copy through Instafreebie or BookFunnel if you don't want to email these files yourself. Readers can follow your link and download the file format of their choice. If you have a paid plan, you can collect email addresses at the same time.

Or hire a blog tour company to do the work for you. You'll have a choice of reviews, guest posts, spotlights and interviews. Here are some of the popular sites:

Great Escapes – https://www.escapewithdollycas.com/great-escapes-virtual-book-tours/
Partners in Crime – http://www.partnersincrimetours.net/
Goddess Fish Promotions – http://www.goddessfish.com/

Giveaways are another method of gaining reviews. Check out LibraryThing giveaways or offer your own Rafflecopter contest.

Join a multi-author free book giveaway as another way to attract readers. See more on this below. Or put your title on sale for a limited period of time and advertise widely. Hopefully you'll get some reviews out of the resultant downloads.

Be wary of getting all five-star reviews from your friends and family. It's best to get honest mixed reviews, and these will happen as word about your book gets around.

If you offer a title on iBooks directly, you can request up to 250 free review codes. Go to iTunes Connect and click on My Books. Click on a book title. Look for a button in the upper right corner that says Promo Codes. Offer them to reviewers and book bloggers or to readers who agree to review your book.

Same goes for ACX when you do an audiobook through their service. Audible sends you 25 review codes, but you can ask for more after these are depleted.

You may wonder if too many giveaways will affect sales. Probably the benefits of getting more reviews outweigh this risk. You can experiment and see what works for you.

You can also do book giveaways on Goodreads, but these now come with a price. Amazon also offers its own version of a giveaway. So opportunities abound. But even with these freebies, it may be hard finding readers to take them and even harder to get them to post a review. The best way for this to work is to produce on a consistent basis and build your repertoire. Also make sure your book shines with professional polish.

When readers post a review, add their name and contact info to a private reviewer list so you can personally offer them a copy of your next title. Do the same for cooperative bloggers and reviewers. Find more by putting "book reviewer" into the search feature of your social media sites or by looking at sources of review quotes on books similar to yours. Remember to thank the reviewers for the time they spent reading your work.

In other words, do your homework. Finding reviewers takes some digging, but consider this task an essential part of your marketing efforts.

Mailing Lists

It's important to collect your own mailing list in case your social media sites disappear overnight or they block your account. You can segregate these addresses into multiple lists for different purposes. For example, you might send an advance release notice to Booksellers and Librarians. Or you might address Fans only with a giveaway offer. I suggest you use a mass email system such as MailChimp or VerticalResponse. This streamlines the process and makes it easier while meeting privacy regulations that affect subscribers.

How do you get names? Exchange business cards at writers' conferences, because writers are readers, too. Bring a sign-up sheet to your in-person events. Put your call to action in the front and back material of your books. Have an opt-in link on all your sites and in your signature line. Most importantly, get the person's consent and document it through whichever method you choose.

Giveaways with other authors offer a way to increase your list, although here you'll get some prize junkies who unsubscribe down the road. That's okay because the contest still raises your exposure. These cost a fee to join. Watch for announcements of these events on your social media sites and follow the source. Ask other authors what places they recommend. I've used Authors Cross-Promotion and Ryan Zee's BookSweeps services. If you join Instafreebie or BookFunnel, these offer joint giveaways along with reader sign-ups. Or do your own giveaways via Rafflecopter.

Once you establish a newsletter template, you can cut and paste each time to avoid starting over from scratch. I create my newsletter content in Word and then transfer the material into my online template. This way, I keep a copy for my files. When it's time to write the next newsletter, I bring up the last one and swap in the new information, then save it as a new file.

Later, you can get into drip campaigns, landing pages, and automated replies, but master the basics first. Entice readers to sign up by offering bonus content as an incentive, such as a free short story, a novella, or a first-in-series free book.

How often should you send a newsletter? Some authors send them monthly. Others do a quarterly posting. Or you can choose to send one whenever you have a new release or other news to share. As for content, include new release info, cover reveals, upcoming appearances, signing events, awards, contests and giveaways, bargain book days, recent blog posts, and social media links. As exclusives for your subscribers, offer recipe or craft tips, deleted scenes, epilogues, interviews with your sleuth, scenes with minor characters, or even book-related puzzles. A book club discussion guide is always welcome.

Your personal newsletter keeps you in touch with readers who want to hear from you. It's the best way to reach fans directly and allows you to retain control over your mailing list. If the social media sites ever shut down, you'll still be able to contact your readers.

Social Media

While you are writing the book, note any possible blog topics in a separate file. This can include inspirational anecdotes, research highlights, character profiles, or notes on the writing process. Then you'll have a handy topic list if you do a virtual book tour.

Make sure you have a professional website including a welcome page, book info, list of appearances, online press kit, printable book list, social media links, biography (in third person with short and long versions), contact info, and buy links. Refresh your content often. Consider having your site designed in WordPress so you can update it yourself, or try one of the free sites that are easy to use.

Establish a platform via blogging and a presence on Facebook. Link your social media accounts to each other. Make sure you have an Amazon Author Page and link your blog to it. Twitter, Instagram, Pinterest, LinkedIn and other sites are useful as well. Start with the one your target audience populates and then expand your reach from there.

Remember the word "social." These sites allow you to interact with fans, ask questions, share interesting articles, and show your personal side. Mix in your experiences regarding hobbies, travels, food, or whatever excites you, but be careful not to reveal anything you don't want to go public. Think in terms of quarters. One fourth of your posts should be to support your colleagues; one fourth to share industry news; another quarter to promote your books; and finally, add in your personal posts to complete the equation. Eventually, you'll find a balance that works best for you.

Consider joining an author "lifeboat team" and helping each other with cross promotion. I belong to Booklover's Bench (https://bookloversbench.com/) where we run monthly contests and offer weekly blog posts. Plus, we tweet and share each other's posts as much as possible. There are lots of author groups out there, so check them out, too. Consider putting your own team together. Invite authors who are social media savvy and who offer newsletters to their fans.

As you become more advanced in social media, you can set up automated tweets, schedule your posts in advance, and utilize other tricks to save time.

Planning a Book Launch

Once you or your publisher sets a date for your new release, you can start planning ahead for the big day. You'll need to begin months earlier and get your pieces lined up ahead of time. Preparing for a new release can be a full-time marketing job, so I'd advise you to set aside a few weeks to get everything done. Here's a basic countdown schedule to act as a guideline.

4 to 6 months ahead

Prepare your story blurbs and tag lines.

Update the author biography on your website. Have a short and long bio along with a separate speaker introduction.

Send out advance reading copies to reviewers and bloggers.

Announce the launch date in your newsletter and on your social media sites.

Schedule a virtual blog tour.

Reserve ad space in trade journals, e-magazines, and online reader sites.

Set up speaking engagements and signings.

Consider doing a Pinterest story board.

2 to 4 months ahead

Send out a press release about the new release and include signing dates.

Do a Cover Reveal once your book is available for pre-order.

Write a page full of tweets and Facebook posts about the new release.

Create your book trailer (optional) and add to social media sites.

Write guest blog articles and interviews for your virtual book tour.
Run contests or giveaways with your ARCs as prizes.
Order print promo materials and swag for conferences.
Consider if you want to put another book in your series on sale during the window of your book launch.

1 to 2 months ahead

Set a book launch party date, time and place. Here's an example of the online site I share with author Maggie Toussaint: https://www.facebook.com/NewReleaseParty/. Other authors might invite their writer friends to participate. Note what appeals to you and use these elements in planning your own book party.
Write the party posts, determine the prizes, and schedule all posts ahead of time.
Create memes for your launch party and the new release.
Send out "Save the Date" notices. Treat the launch as an "event" and broadcast it on your social media sites and to your influential contacts.
Schedule a newsletter and blog to post on the launch date.
Update your website with reviews as they come in. If time permits, thank each reviewer.
Write a book club discussion guide (optional).
Post the first chapter on your website.
Put excerpts on your blog to entice readers to want more.

Do as much of this work in advance as you can. This is simplifying all the effort a book launch entails, but being prepared relieves some of the stress as your book birthday approaches. You should also think about your book launch schedule going forward. You'll want to allow sufficient time between releases so as not to flood reviewers with requests and to give them enough time to read your book. If your new releases are too close together, you'll be bombarding your social media sites as well with too many promotional posts.

Give yourself and your readers a rest and use the time in between books to write blog posts for the next release.

Other authors may have success doing back-to-back releases, but is this comfortable for you? If you're published with a traditional press, you won't have this problem. But if you are an indie or hybrid author, consider the timing. Try to space things out so you can breathe in between book launches. Readers won't forget about you if you remain active with excerpts, posts about your life and the writing process, and do the other items we've mentioned above.

In Conclusion

There's a lot more we could discuss about marketing, but first you need to finish your book. Keep your eyes open and observe what your fellow writers are doing in terms of promotion. Join author groups and online forums and do your homework. There's no magic bullet for a runaway bestseller. Hard work is required to get your name out there. Think more in terms of author recognition as a goal rather than book sales. Sales will grow as readers get to know you. Watch for opportunities, keep learning, and write more books.

Chapter Seventeen – Final Words

Writing a cozy mystery is a complex task. You'll find that much of the story will sprout from your subconscious once you start mulling over the bits and pieces you've gathered. Somehow, the puzzle fits together in the end. Your challenge is to create an appealing sleuth, surround her with an engaging supporting cast, and then develop the suspects. Victim, crime, and villain will soon fall into place. Mix in your clues, figure out how to reveal them to your sleuth, and you're on your way toward the grand finale. Satisfaction will come when a reader writes to you and says, "Your story kept me guessing until the end."

Chapter Eighteen – Resources

Bouchercon: http://www.bouchercon.com/
Cozy Mystery List: https://www.cozy-mystery.com/
Crime Scene Writer: https://groups.io/g/Crimescenewriter2
Florida Chapter of MWA: http://www.mwaflorida.org/
Independent Mystery Booksellers Association: http://www.mysterybooksellers.com
In Reference to Murder: http://www.inreferencetomurder.com/
International Thriller Writers: http://thrillerwriters.org/
Just the Facts, Ma'am: https://thoniehevron.wordpress.com/
Killer Nashville: http://www.killernashville.com/
Kiss of Death RWA: http://www.rwakissofdeath.org/
Left Coast Crime: http://www.leftcoastcrime.org
Malice Domestic: http://malicedomestic.org/index.html
Murder Must Advertise: http://www.murdermustadvertise.com/
Mystery Writers of America: http://www.mysterywriters.org
Sisters in Crime: http://www.sistersincrime.org
SleuthFest: http://sleuthfest.com
The Crime Fiction Writer's Forensic Blog: http://writersforensicsblog.wordpress.com/
The Graveyard Shift: http://www.leelofland.com/wordpress/
The Kill Zone: https://killzoneblog.com/
Thrillerfest: http://www.thrillerfest.com/
Writers Police Academy: http://www.writerspoliceacademy.com

Acknowledgments

With gratitude to my beta readers and fellow authors whose knowledge and expertise helped me improve this book: Rachel Blalock Bateman, James. M. Jackson, Alyssa Maxwell, Terry Odell, Elizabeth Penney, and Penny Thomas.

I am deeply grateful for your time and effort on my behalf. This expanded edition wouldn't have been possible without your valued input.

Thanks to Judi Fennell from formatting4U.com for the interior layout that gives my work a professional finish.

And special kudos to Patty G. Henderson from Boulevard Photografica for the standout cover design and illustrations. Thank you to a highly talented artist.

Author's Note

If you find this book to be useful, please help spread the word. This is the best way for new readers to find my work. Here are some suggestions:

Write an online customer review.
Post about my work on your social media sites and online forums.
Recommend this book to your writing groups and workshops.
If you teach fiction writing, mention this resource to your class.
Gift this book to a writer friend.

For updates on my new releases, giveaways, special offers and events, join my reader list at https://nancyjcohen.com/newsletter. Free Book Sampler for new subscribers.

About the Author

As a former registered nurse, Nancy J. Cohen helped people with their physical aches and pains, but she longed to soothe their troubles in a different way. The siren call of storytelling lured her from nursing into the exciting world of fiction. Wishing she could wield a curling iron with the same skill as crafting a story, she created hairdresser Marla Vail as a stylist with a nose for crime and a knack for exposing people's secrets.

Titles in the Bad Hair Day Mysteries have made the IMBA bestseller list, been selected by *Suspense Magazine* as best cozy mystery, won a Readers' Favorite gold medal, and earned third place in the Arizona Literary Awards. Nancy has also written the instructional guide, *Writing the Cozy Mystery*. Her imaginative romances have proven popular with fans as well. These books have won the HOLT Medallion and Best Book in Romantic SciFi/Fantasy at *The Romance Reviews*.

A featured speaker at libraries, conferences, and community events, Nancy is listed in *Contemporary Authors, Poets & Writers*, and *Who's Who in U.S. Writers, Editors, & Poets*. When not busy writing, she enjoys fine dining, cruising, visiting Disney World, and shopping. Contact her at nancy@nancyjcohen.com

Follow Nancy Online

Website: https://nancyjcohen.com
Blog: https://nancyjcohen.wordpress.com

Facebook: https://www.facebook.com/NancyJCohenAuthor
Twitter: https://www.twitter.com/nancyjcohen
Goodreads: https://www.goodreads.com/nancyjcohen
Pinterest: https://pinterest.com/njcohen/
Linked In: https://www.linkedin.com/in/nancyjcohen
Google Plus: https://plus.google.com/+NancyJCohen/
Instagram: https://instagram.com/nancyjcohen
Booklover's Bench: https://bookloversbench.com
BookBub: https://www.bookbub.com/authors/nancy-j-cohen

Books by Nancy J. Cohen

Bad Hair Day Mysteries
Permed to Death
Hair Raiser
Murder by Manicure
Body Wave
Highlights to Heaven
Died Blonde
Dead Roots
Perish by Pedicure
Killer Knots
Shear Murder
Hanging by a Hair
Peril by Ponytail
Haunted Hair Nights (Novella)
Facials Can Be Fatal
Hair Brained
Hairball Hijinks (Short Story)
Trimmed to Death

Anthologies
"Three Men and a Body" in Wicked Women Whodunit

The Drift Lords Series
Warrior Prince
Warrior Rogue
Warrior Lord

Science Fiction Romances
Keeper of the Rings
Silver Serenade

The Light-Years Series
Circle of Light
Moonlight Rhapsody
Starlight Child

Nonfiction
Writing the Cozy Mystery

For More Details, visit http://nancyjcohen.com/books/

Made in the USA
Lexington, KY
05 April 2019